TALES OF LIVERPOOL

MURDER   MAYHEM   MYSTERY

RICHARD WHITTINGTON-EGAN

THE GALLERY PRESS
LEIGHTON ROAD, NESTON, SOUTH WIRRAL

ISBN 0 900389 10 9
Published by Gallery Press 1985
© Richard Whittington-Egan
Printed by Leemancolour Ltd., Neston, South Wirral.

2

Back in the days when the Beatles would still pop into Ye Cracke in Rice Street to take a friendly ale with me, I was paying a young man's court to the fickle jade of the Mersey. I wrote two love chronicles of our on-off affair—*Liverpool Colonnade* and *Liverpool Roundabout*. Oh, I was a knight-errant then, pricking in fancy my milk-white palfrey through the stone forest and down the avenues of my imagination. And such imaginings! I saw the Liver birds take wing against a low lying hunter's moon . . . the chimney-masted tangle of sky-riding roof-tops looking at dusk like the decks of ships at swaying anchor . . . I heard the golden and porcelained names on windows singing the old crafts' songs and lullabies of trade . . . I lurked around the Western bazaar counters in the lit grottoes of the shops . . . I rode the overhead railway and the Noah's Ark tramcars . . . watched the glittering city slip over the horizon's edge into the purple pomp of night—and out again into the watered-milk light of another dawn. Both I and the Liverpool of which I wrote have grown up, grown different. We have played weather-vanes to the wind of change. And yet we are still the same at heart. The fresh wind blowing across the river and over my city's wild hilltop still whispers the old tales to those who are willing to listen . . . a light still burns in Paradise Street . . .

CONTENTS

1. WHEN SPRING-HEELED JACK VISITED EVERTON

It is more than eighty years ago now since Spring-Heeled Jack, the Leaping Terror, set the good people of Everton trembling in their houses. Until quite recently, echoes of that old fear lingered in the memories of elderly folk who had lived most of their lives in that part of Liverpool and remembered being told by their mothers, "Spring-Heeled Jack will get you if you don't behave yourself."

It was on a late September's day in the year 1904 that that legendary figure of fear dropped in on the startled Evertonians, and hundreds of people watched in fascinated horror while the fantastic creature hopped up and down the length of William Henry Street. The extraordinary spectacle continued for some ten or twelve minutes with "Jack" making gigantic bounds—some of which are said to have exceeded twenty-five feet—from roadway to rooftop, until finally, after leaping clean over the houses from Stitt Street into Haigh Street and then back across the roofs to Salisbury Street, he vanished never to be seen again.

Admittedly, to modern ears this sounds an extremely tall story, and, were it an isolated incident, one might be tempted to dismiss it as an exceptionally vivid instance of mass hallucination. But, as a matter of fact, it was the culmination of something like eighty-seven years of similar reports from every part of the country which gave rise to a sensation in Victorian and Edwardian England that bade fair to rival the flying-saucer furore of recent years.

The first definite evidence of the existence of Spring-Heeled Jack comes from the south of England—from London. The year is 1837. At that date, vague tales concerning the "Jumping Man" had been current for perhaps fifteen or twenty years. Nothing really concrete emerged, however, until after the Lord Mayor of London had instructed the Lambeth police to investigate certain complaints which he had received concerning mysterious attacks upon persons living in the vicinity of Barnes Common. In the course of their enquiries the police interviewed a Miss Jane Alsop, and from her obtained first-hand details of a brutal attack by "a creature of hideous and frightful aspect."

Twenty-five-year-old Jane Alsop lived with her father and two sisters in a lonely house in Bearbird Lane between Bow and Oldford. Shortly before 9 o'clock one dark December evening in 1837, there came a violent ringing at the front-gate bell. Miss Alsop answered it herself and found there a tall man enveloped from head to foot in a cloak. He told her that he was a police-officer. "For God's sake bring me a light," he gasped breathlessly, "for we have caught Spring-Heeled Jack in the lane." She fetched a lighted candle and handed it to the stranger. No sooner had she done so than he threw back his cloak. What she saw petrified her. The man's body was encased in a tightly-fitting garment of some kind of white oilskin and on his head was a large helmet beneath which his eyes blazed like fireballs. Without another word he leapt upon her, vomiting blue and white flames from his mouth, and began to tear at her dress and body with sharp, metallic claws. The girl screamed loudly and managed to break away, but her attacker pursued her and catching her, just as she reached the steps of the house, commenced clawing her face, neck and hair. Luckily, one of her sisters had heard the screams and came running to the rescue, whereupon the man bounded off into the darkness.

Mr. Alsop and his daughters subsequently made depositions regarding this incident at Lambeth Police-Court. A few days later their story received striking corroboration before the same magistrates from a respectable young man named Scales, who owned a butchering business in Narrow Street, Limehouse, and lived on the opposite side of Barnes Common. A day or two before the Bearbird Lane attack, Scales had been visited one evening by his two young sisters. They left his home at about 8-30, and a few minutes after their departure he heard loud screams. Rushing out, Scales almost collided with his sister Margaret as she came stumbling out of nearby Green Alley, shrieking and pointing fearfully into the blackness behind her. There, he found his other sister, Lucy, lying moaning on the ground. When they had sufficiently recovered, the girls recounted how they had seen a very tall man swathed in a cloak and carrying a lamp or bull's-eye lantern in front of him. Suddenly, he had rushed at Lucy and spurted blue flames from his mouth into her face momentarily blinding her. She fell to the ground in terror and he moved as if to attack her, but when Margaret began to scream he turned, and, jumping clean over a high wall, disappeared from sight.

So it was, with these two cases, that Spring-Heeled Jack made his official début.

Naturally, the newspapers of the time accorded wide publicity to both incidents, with the result that people gave Barnes Common a wide berth after dark, and there were consequently no further reports of Spring-Heeled Jack having been seen in that district. Indeed, for several years there was a lull in the "Jumping Man's" activities.

In 1845, however, another scare occurred, this time in the Ealing and Hanwell areas of London, where women and children going along lonely roads at night were frightened out of their wits by a weird figure in a white gown and a dark shawl which they saw leaping over hedges and walls, shrieking and groaning as it went. Once again the name of Spring-Heeled Jack was whispered uneasily from ear to ear. The local police were called in and this time they managed to catch the "phantom," who turned out

6

to be a Brentford butcher named Richard Bradford. This man was an inveterate practical joker and, brought before the Brentford magistrates, he was lucky enough to be discharged with a caution.

Throughout the '50's and '60's, Spring-Heeled Jack scares continued to take place all over the country. Now, the Springing Horror seemed to have forsaken London and accounts of his appearances began to arrive from Warwickshire, Staffordshire, Lancashire, Lincolnshire, Worcestershire, Middlesex and Surrey. By the '70's, however, he had returned to the capital, and there were innumerable reports of his activities from the more remote districts of London as well as a steady stream from the provinces.

In 1877 there occurred an incident which must rate as one of Jack's most convincing performances. It was a summer's night of brilliant moonlight and Private John Regan was on sentry-go at the gates of the powder-magazine of Aldershot's North Camp. Regan was standing at ease in his sentry-box when he heard a harsh, grating noise as if someone were dragging a heavy metal object along the ground. Rifle cocked, he stepped out of his box and peered up and down the moonlit length of road. There was nothing to be seen. About thirty feet away on the opposite side of the gates the other sentry was still in his box. He did not seem to have been disturbed. Regan concluded that his imagination must have been playing tricks on him, but as he turned to go back to his box he felt the icy touch of an invisible hand upon his cheek. That was not imagination. With a cry of fear, he dropped his rifle, and, at that, the second sentry came running out of his box. Then, as the two men stood together in the moonlight, a large, dark shape passed over their heads and landed noiselessly at the roadside. A fantastic figure in a tight-fitting suit and a queer, shining helmet, it stood glaring at them. Regan levelled his rifle and, after shakily challenging the creature, took careful aim at it. Unharmed, it leapt into the air and, swooping down low over Regan's head, belched a stream of blue flame into his face. After that both soldiers fired several shots at it without effect until, overcome by panic, they fled from their posts.

It is interesting to note that the soldiers' description of what they saw—a tall, thin figure, wearing a tight-fitting suit and gleaming helmet, with glowing red eyes and blue flames issuing from its mouth—was couched in terms amazingly similar to those used by Jane Alsop forty years before.

The curious imperviousness to bullets of the Aldershot phantom was also manifest in the October and November of 1877, when Spring-Heeled Jack appeared near Newport in Lincolnshire. His costume this time was described by eye-witnesses as resembling a sheepskin with a peculiar tail, and he is said to have had huge, pointed ears. He jumped onto a cottage roof and ran over the housetops. Pursued by a mob, he leapt onto Newport's old Roman arch, and a man with a gun promptly fired at him. A few minutes later, he was shot at again as he ran along the walls of the New Barracks, but the bullets had not the slightest effect on him, and presently he bounded off as silently as he had come.

And so his career continued through the '80's and '90's and into the present century. In 1888, when the appalling series of "Ripper Murders" set a grip of terror about the heart of London's East End, there were many who thought that Jack-the-Ripper and Spring-Heeled Jack were one and the same.

Round about this time, too, many stories were circulating regarding the appearance of the phantom in the south end of Liverpool.

He was said to have been seen springing from the top of the reservoir in High Park Street and jumping over high garden walls in the neighbourhood of St. Michael's-in-the-Hamlet. He was even reported from as far afield as the vicinity of Childwall Abbey.

An elderly man, still living, has also told how, one night in 1888, when he and a number of his fellow-members of Everton's St. Francis Xavier's Boys' Guild were playing in the school-room, someone came rushing in with the news that the dread Spring-Heeled Jack was in Shaw Street. Out into Haigh Street ran the boys, and up William Henry Street. When, however, they reached Shaw Street, they saw no sign of the weird creature, although an excited crowd told them that he was crouched on the steeple of a nearby church.

The new century was but four years old when Jack made his final bow, and the place of his last recorded appearance was, as we have said, Liverpool.

Since that distant September day when the Leaping Terror capered grotesquely up and down William Henry Street, he has never been seen again.

Many theories have been advanced seeking to explain away the undoubted presence of the "Jumping Man," but the question as to whether or not it really was a hostile species of phantom has never been settled. There have been suggestions that he was an insane circus acrobat-cum-fire-eater, who, clad in a costume provided with animal claws and a bullet-proof vest, painted his eyes with phosphorus and attached powerful springs to his heels. Some people believe that what the soldiers saw at Aldershot was a large, crested eagle in the moonlight. Others, hazard that Spring-Heeled Jack was a huge kangaroo brought from Australia by a crazed animal-trainer, who taught it to attack women when turned loose in a one-piece suit, a cloak and a helmet! There are even those who incline to the view that he was a visitor from Space. This, they argue, would account for his astounding leaping proclivities because he would be adapted to the requirements of life on a greater-gravity planet. Likewise, differences in physical constitution would probably enable him to live longer on earth and might well explain the flame-like emanations from his mouth. But, after all these years, the mystery remains as profound as on that December night in 1837, when Jane Alsop first glimpsed her unearthly assailant, and it seems unlikely now that it will ever be resolved, unless, of course, a flying-saucer should happen to land in Everton!

2. CYLINDER OF DEATH

Appropriately enough, it was on Friday the Thirteenth that they made the gruesome discovery: Friday, 13th July, 1945, to be precise. It was a little group of children playing on a blitzed-site at the corner of Fulford Street and Great Homer Street, that first stumbled upon the cylinder. It lay among the spilled red bricks of the waste land, strangely black-looking in the bright sunlight. A game of hide-and-seek was in progress and the fun was at its height. Nine-year-old Tommy Lawless crouched, laughing, behind the cylinder. "Ready!" he shouted. And then, he saw the boot. It was projecting from between the compressed, leaden lips of the open end of the cylinder. He called to his playmates. Excitedly, they gathered round while Tommy eased the boot from the narrow gap. All at once there was a gasp of horror, for, as the boot came out, they saw within the dark interior of the cylinder the stark, white bone of a human leg. Even upon that brilliant July morning, so tight a grip of fear fastened about those young hearts, that, in a single instant, they overcame a lifetime's nurturing in fear of "bobbies" and ran helter-skelter in search of one.

It was just 11-45 a.m., when a terrified boy ran up to Police-Constable Robert Baillie who was on duty at the junction of Great Homer Street and Kirkdale Road, and breathlessly told him of his discovery. The officer accompanied the lad to the waste ground, examined the cylinder and had it removed to the mortuary.

That was the beginning.

The mystery opened its dark bud in the City Morgue. When, at 1-10 p.m., the cylinder was officially deposited in the mortuary, it must have seemed just another routine job. Certainly, there was nothing to indicate just how strange a corpse lay hidden within it. Its arrival was duly recorded and it was prosaically described as a riveted, sheet-iron cylinder, approximately 6 feet 9 inches long and 18¾ inches in diameter, sealed at one end with an iron lid, riveted in position, and the other end closed by pressing together. At about 3 o'clock that afternoon an engineer was sent for and the cylinder was cut open with an acetylene blowlamp. What was then revealed must have astonished even the accustomed eyes of Dr. Charles Vincent Harrison, at that time senior lecturer in pathology at Liverpool University, who had come to perform a post-mortem examination on behalf of the coroner. There, stretched upon a rough bed of sacking, his head resting on a kind of pillow formed of a brick covered with a sack, was the corpse of a man clad in tattered Victorian clothing. He wore a braid-edged morning-coat with cloth-covered buttons, narrow, striped trousers and elastic-sided boots. They laid the cadaver upon a dissecting-slab and there, amid the clean, white tiles, Dr. Harrison began his autopsy. What he found left him in no doubt that the body had been dead for a long time. The remains were those of an adult male, the state of whose bones indicated that he had been more than twenty-five years of age when he died. On the other hand, since the teeth were fairly well preserved and a quantity of hair adhering to the skull was brown and not grey, it was unlikely that he was of more than middle age. Harrison calculated his height as having been about 6 feet and added that there was no way of ascertaining the cause of death.

Naturally, this extraordinary discovery excited considerable curiosity when it was reported in the press. On the face of it, it seemed impossible to learn anything more about the man in the iron cylinder. Who was he? How came he to be in that great metal canister? These were questions which appeared likely to remain unanswered. But the police are accustomed to having to find answers to apparently hopeless questions and their determination, together with what the coroner was subsequently to call "the astonishing perseverance of the Liverpool C.I.D.", led to the unearthing of certain facts which went a long way towards solving a unique mystery.

The first thing the police did was to call in that great forensic expert, Dr. J. B. Firth, director of Preston's Home Office Forensic Science Laboratory. Dr. Firth came to Liverpool and made an exhaustive examination. In the main he agreed with Dr. Harrison's conclusions, though he put the man's height at about 5 feet 7 inches. He took possession of certain clues including a number of keys, a penknife, a gold signet-ring, set with a bloodstone and bearing the hall-mark for London, 1859, and two monthly-diaries for July 1884, and June 1885, respectively. Most important of all, however, Firth recovered from the tail pocket of the right half of the morning-coat, a small wad of papers. This wad was a solid mass of adipocere (a peculiar waxen substance which forms during the decomposition of bodies, especially when they have been in contact with moisture) and it was only after a great deal of work, which involved treating the bundle with organic solvents and carefully separating its constituents with a spatula, that Firth was able to isolate and render legible thirteen documents. They proved to be the vital clue, for many of them related to T. C. Williams & Co., of Leeds Street, Liverpool. They also included a postcard addressed to Mr. T. C. Williams himself.

Meanwhile, on July 19th, 1945, the inquest was opened by the Liverpool Coroner, then Dr. G. C. Mort, and was adjourned for one month. On August 16th it was further adjourned to August 31st to enable the police to complete certain inquiries.

Once he had the name T. C. Williams to work with, Detective-

Inspector (later Chief-Inspector) John William Morris, who, under Superintendent (later Assistant Chief-Constable) A. W. Fothergill, was in charge of investigations, really got busy. He found that in the year 1883 there was a firm of Oil Merchants, Paint & Varnish Manufacturers trading under the name of T. C. Williams & Co., and with the business address of 18-20 Leeds Street. The principal of this firm was a Mr. Thomas Cregeen Williams, who lived at what was then 29 Clifton Road, Anfield. Williams had originally been a commercial traveller and had later set up in business on his own account. He was born somewhere about 1830, and married Elizabeth Lea, who died at 29 Clifton Road, aged 42, and was buried, as Elizabeth Williams, at Anfield Cemetery at 10 a.m., on 25th May, 1878. There was one child of the marriage, Thomas Lea Cregeen Williams, born about November, 1858. Inspector Morris also discovered that in 1884 a T. C. Williams, with a paint works in Leeds Street, was undergoing an examination, handled by a well-known firm of Liverpool accountants, in connection with his business. This Mr. Williams was extremely worried over his affairs. Significantly, maybe, Inspector Morris could trace no record of the death of T. C. Williams, nor, after 1884, could he find any mention of the firm in any Liverpool trades directory. Furthermore, a careful search failed to reveal any official bankruptcy.

There, matters had perforce to remain, and, on August 31st, 1945, the coroner closed the inquest by recording an open verdict on the death of an unknown man.

That the "Unknown Man" was Thomas Cregeen Williams seems more than probable: that his death took place *circa* July 4th, 1885, is generally accepted, but the cause of that death remains a complete mystery. The bones and clothes were analysed by Dr. Firth for poisons but none were found. Nevertheless, the experts felt that there was a strong likelihood of the man's having committed suicide. In charity, however, we must not entirely dismiss the possibility that Williams—if it *was* Williams—finding himself in financial difficulties, was keeping away from home in order to evade his creditors. He may have crawled into the cylinder to sleep and in so doing shut out the air and asphyxiated himself. It could well be that his disappearance caused no sensation at the time, as in those days it was not unusual for debtors to flee their creditors by boarding a ship and working their passage abroad.

The whole story is a bizarre one teeming with fascinating possibilities. In 1945 I was in Italy, and the circumstances first came to my attention through a batch of news-cuttings which were sent out to me. I was profoundly interested then and I have remained so ever since. Back in England in 1949, I listened to an intriguing radio play, "The Black Cap Has to Wait," by H. R. Jeans, based upon the Liverpool cylinder case.

But ten years had to elapse before I was able to fulfil a long-standing ambition to make a few inquiries of my own.

In a quiet street off Stanley Road, I found Mr. William Pemberton, who used to be the caretaker at the Methodist Church in Boundary Street East. Mr. Pemberton is seventy-nine and he is the man who first saw the cylinder in the summer of 1943. "The American soldiers were clearing the site at the back of our church," he said. "There was a large bomb-crater and the cylinder was in the crater with the open end downwards. I saw the spade of a mechanical navvy crush the cylinder in its efforts to dislodge it. About a couple of months later another navvy managed to get the cylinder out and laid it on the level ground. The boys used to roll it about all over the place and I have seen gipsies sitting on it in the sunshine making their artificial flowers."

By a stroke of good fortune I succeeded in finding Tommy Lawless. He was then nineteen, a tall, dark-haired young man, and he went into the army the week after I met him. He remembers finding the cylinder because when he saw the boot sticking out of it he thought that he was in luck. "I'd never had a pair of boots in my life," he told me, "and when I saw a smashing pair like that I thought my days of running round barefoot were at an end." Tommy took me along to Fulford Street and showed me where the cylinder used to lie. The blitzed-site had disappeared and a bright crop of pre-fabs stood where it had once been. Mr. and Mrs. Robert Foy's home covered the exact spot where Tommy made his alarming discovery, and when I told them about it Mrs. Foy said with a laugh, "Well, it's no wonder that we've had no luck, is it?" Still, she was very proud of the spick and span little house and I don't think she would like to have left it.

The next day I went to see Dr. Firth at his Preston laboratory and had a long talk with him about the case. He had preserved portions of the original documents which his skill and patience extracted from the fatty mass and which did so much to dispel the mystery. He also had a series of lantern-slides illustrating various aspects of his investigations and was kind enough to give me a little lecture all to myself on how he read the hidden clues in the cylinder.

I also visited the late Chief-Inspector J. W. Morris and heard from his own lips many interesting sidelights on what he described to me as "one of the most interesting cases that I have ever had to deal with." At the time though, he had his leg pulled quite a bit about it. "You worried about the question of identity?" asked one of his friends. The inspector admitted that he was rather. "It's obvious," came the reply, "Nothing to worry about. The fellow is undoubtedly a boiler-maker who got wrapped up in his work!"

And last of all I went to Anfield Cemetery where an obliging young lady showed me what is perhaps the most fascinating of all the things I saw in the course of my search. She produced a great, dusty, blue volume, its leather binding crumbling with age. It was an old receipt book which people signed more than a hundred years ago, when they received the deeds of a grave. And there, over the date 21st December, 1878, in brown and fading ink, I beheld the name Thomas Cregeen Williams. Unreasonably, perhaps, I was suddenly certain that it was the autograph of the man in the cylinder.

3. THE HOPE STREET CELLAR OF HORRORS

In the twilight of an October evening in the year 1826 a cart is lurching its way through the gathering gloom of the George's Dock Passage.

Upon this cart are three large Newfoundland oil casks which are prominently labelled "Bitter Salts."

The eyes of the driver seek among the flickers of dockside lamps for the smack which bears upon her bows the name *Latona*, for it is his business to deliver the casks to that vessel. In his pocket there reposes a note which is addressed to the Carron Company and which reads as follows:—

> "Please ship on board the *Latona*
> three casks of bitter salts,
> from Mr. Brown, agent, Liverpool,
> to Mr. G. H. Ironson, Edinburgh.
> (signed) J. Brown."

It is not long before the carter has discovered the *Latona*, one of the smacks which trade between Liverpool and Leith, which is lying in the George's Dock Passage, and, his mission accomplished, is rumbling complacently homewards. At that time he has no knowledge of the strange cargo which he has just delivered, and little thinks that what seems to him to be the end of the transaction is, in reality, but the beginning of an extremely unsavoury mystery. He will hear more of it, much more, but meanwhile he does not know this, it is getting late and he turns his back upon the darkening waterfront.

Nor is the carter the only one anxious to quit the docks. It has been a long day and the crew of the *Latona* feel the urge to abandon ship and escape into the more convivial atmosphere of the Paradise Street taverns. So the casks are hastily slipped betwixt decks, time enough to stow them away tomorrow.

Next morning, however, when the sailors came to deal with the casks they were so overcome by the terrible stench which they gave off, that it was decided that the matter had best be reported to the master. Captain Walker examined the offending casks at once, and, drawing out a plug of straw which had been stuffed into a small hole in the side of one of the barrels, he released so unmistakable an odour of corruption that he made up his mind there and then to investigate further. He ordered one of the bungs to be started and, upon introducing his hand into the barrel, the Captain was horrified to encounter, not the chemical substance which he had anticipated, but the soft tell-tale contours of a human body. Naturally, he immediately sent a message to the Carron Company telling them of his gruesome discovery, and they promptly communicated with

15

the police. The casks were removed forthwith to the Old City Deadhouse in Chapel Street, and when opened they proved to contain no less than eleven human bodies packed in salt—bitter salt, indeed!

The police set to work at once to trace the carter who had borne this grisly freight to the *Latona*. The investigation was undertaken by an active officer named Robert Boughey, and in a remarkably short space of time he had managed to track down the carter. His name was George Leech and he had a strange story to tell. He had, he said, been with his brother's cart at the stand at the Dry Dock on the previous Monday afternoon. Sometime between three and four o'clock he was approached by a tall, stout man with black whiskers. The stranger, who spoke with a thick Scottish accent, had offered him the sum of two shillings if he would deliver three casks to the *Latona* for him. Leech had agreed to this proposition and was directed to take his cart to Number 8 Hope Street. There, he was met by two men who brought the barrels from the cellar and gave him a hand to life them onto his cart. That same evening he had transported them to the ship which he understood was bound for Leith. And that, said Leech, was as much as he knew of the matter.

After hearing this tale, Boughey went straight to the house in Hope Street. He found it occupied by the Reverend James Macgowan who ran a small private school there. In reply to the officer's inquiries, Macgowan said that he had let his cellar in the previous January to a Mr. John Henderson, a native of Greenock, who had told him that he was a cooper by trade and was engaged in the export of fish-oil. Boughey then asked for the key of the cellar, but Macgowan replied that it was not in his possession. Thereupon, Boughey took a crowbar and announced his intention of breaking the door down. Macgowan became excited and ordered him to desist from damaging his property. When Boughey seemed disinclined to desist, the reverend gentleman threatened to bring an action against him, but the intrepid Boughey was not to be dissuaded and the door was burst open to reveal in that dusky subterranean place, a scene of horror such as might have been wrung from the tortured imagination of an Edgar Allan Poe. Scattered about in a number of casks and sacks, Boughey found the corpses of twenty-two men, women and children. Here, then, was a sinister riddle. How come all these dead bodies to be gathered together in this frightful basement charnel-house?

It was the police-surgeon, Thomas William Davis, who provided the solution. From his examination of the remains he concluded that in every case death had occurred from natural causes, and upon the toe of one young woman he found a significant fragment of thread. This led him to believe that the bodies had been disinterred—probably from the parish cemetery which was situated about a quarter of a mile away from Hope

16

Street, in an area at the foot of what is now Cambridge Street—for it was a common practice in those days to keep the feet of the deceased together by tying the toes. From this small clue, together with the discovery in the cellar of various other pieces of evidence, such as a syringe of the type which anatomists employed to inject hot wax into the veins and arteries of cadavers, he had no hesitation in saying that in the Hope Street basement the police had stumbled upon nothing less than a body-snatchers' warehouse! Moreover, October was that season of the year when the anatomical lectures were just beginning in the Scottish medical schools, and the northern surgeons were always on the look-out for subjects for their dissecting-tables. So vigilantly were the churchyards in Scotland guarded against the depredations of resurrectionists, that the anatomists used to have to send their agents to England, where there was little difficulty in finding men who were quite ready to satisfy their demands at the rate of £10 to £15 per body.

Despite the widespread search which ensued for the Liverpool "sack-'em-up men," Henderson, the main actor in that grim little drama, was never brought to justice. Two other men were arrested however. One, Gillespie, was subsequently discharged, but the other, 25-year-old James Donaldson, later stood trial on the charge of "having conspired with divers other persons, lately at Liverpool, and unlawfully, willfully and indecently disinterred, taken and carried away divers dead bodies." The trial aroused considerable excitement and not a little horror and indignation. When, at one stage in the proceedings, it was described how a huge barrel containing a number of babies soaked in brine had been discovered, an audible shudder passed through the court and the foreman of the jury was taken ill and obliged to make a hasty exit. Donaldson was found guilty, sentenced to twelve months in the Kirkdale House of Correction and ordered to pay a fine of £50.

On November 9th, 1826, a third man, John Ross, was taken into custody for being concerned in the outrage, and also a man named Peter M'Gregor. The circumstances surrounding the arrest are curious. On Saturday, November 4th, a man brought a large box to the White House coach-office in Dale Street. Shortly after his departure, the coach-office book-keeper noticed a very offensive smell coming from the box and, probably recollecting the recent discoveries at Hope Street, he took it upon himself to open the box. Within, was the body of a woman. A day or two later, a man carried a similar box into the Golden Lion Inn, also in Dale Street, which was addressed for forwarding to Edinburgh. The book-keeper, his suspicions thoroughly aroused, managed to detain the man who had brought it until the police arrived. The box was then forced open and, sure enough, yet another human body was disclosed. Both Ross and

M'Gregor were committed for trial, charged with having unlawfully opened graves and carried away dead bodies. They were each sentenced to twelve months imprisonment and each had to pay a fine of £21 to the King.

So ended the case of the Liverpool body-snatchers and, although occasional premature resurrections are recorded as having subsequently taking place here, the Hope Street affair stands unique in the annals of the city as the only instance of the existence in Liverpool of an organised company of body-snatchers for the export of corpses to Scotland.

It is difficult for us in these days of well-ordered medical schools to understand the state of affairs which gave rise to the body-snatchers who once purveyed their gruesome merchandise to the centres of anatomical learning. Prior to 1832, the dissection of human bodies was not legalised in the British Isles, but that law which condemned the procuring of a cavadar for purposes of dissection, nevertheless required all medical candidates to have practical acquaintance with human anatomy. In short, those who would fulfil the law had first to break it! Certain provisions were made in that the scant material from the gallows was handed over to the doctors. But demand was far in excess of supply. To remedy this deficiency, an anatomist would periodically gather about him a band of his heftiest students and sally forth on a grave-rifling expedition. Obviously, a busy anatomist could not find the time to do all his own cadaver-stealing, and there came into being a new "professional" class known variously as "Body-snatchers," "Resurrectionists," "Fishermen" and, most descriptively, as "Sack-'em-up-men."

The majority of "Sack'em-up-men" were blackguards. Often they would sell a body to one anatomist only to steal it back and re-sell it elsewhere. Another ruse was to deliver a drunk in the corpse-sack, pocket the money and disappear before the deception could be discovered. But the body-snatchers did not have it all their own way, and woebetide any unfortunate fisherman who was caught about his ghoulish activities. A mob would soon gather and he was quite likely to be kicked to death.

On the other hand, as long as things went well there was good money in the business and quite reasonable prices could be obtained for such by-products as teeth. In those days there was no National Health Service to provide plastic dentures and dentists were only too pleased to purchase teeth, torn from the mouths of corpses, which were destined to grace the edentulous mouths of unsuspecting, rich patients!

By 1827, the position had reached its unsavoury climax, but the legislators were still more concerned with the problems of fox-hunting than with the dilemma of the doctors. It took a national calamity, a series of the most brutal murders, to stir the national conscience into belated activity.

The echoes of the horror which was aroused by these terrible crimes, which came to be known as the Burke and Hare murders, still sound in the corridors of memory a hundred and twenty-seven years after their perpetrators have answered for their misdeeds. Parliamentary indifference was swept away before the resultant wave of popular fury and the year 1832 saw the passing of the Anatomy Act, which made adequate provisions for the supply of subjects to properly qualified persons. This measure sealed the death-warrant of the body-snatchers. The golden age of the miners of the cemeteries had passed for ever. Gone now is the fear that sacriligeous hands may resurrect our loved ones before the appointed day, and that the flowers planted upon their graves and watered by the tears of the bereaved may bloom above an empty coffin. Nowadays we can look with the detached interest of distance upon such bizarre occurrences as the Hope Street incident, but pausing, perhaps, a moment, to ponder the warning of the baseness of which man is capable when once the lust for gold is roused within him.

4. KILLINGS THAT CHANGED A STREET NAME

You will search the Liverpool street directory in vain for Leveson Street. In the middle of the last century its name was on everyone's lips: today, it has vanished without a trace. What is the strange story that lies behind the disappearance of that once-famous throughfare? The answer is MURDER—for it was murder most foul that took Leveson Street off the map.

In the early afternoon of March 28th, 1849, a terror-stricken errand-boy, running as fast as his little legs would carry him, dashed headlong up Great George Street and into the arms of a patrolling policeman.

"Now then; now then," remonstrated that astonished officer, but a glance at the boy's pale face and wide-staring eyes told him that something was wrong. "What's to do, lad?" he queried in more kindly tones.

"Murder!" gasped the breathless boy.

"Now then ....." the constable began again.

"It's true, Mister. I didn't see her killed but she's dead. You come back with me to Leveson Street and see for yourself."

And so the policeman and the errand-boy went together to Number 20 Leveson Street. What they found there started a sensation which rocked the whole country, setting a finger to the trigger of terror in many a household, particularly in those where lodgings were let to single men.

★   ★   ★   ★

It was sometime during the latter part of 1848 that Captain John Henry Hinrichson, the master of a sailing-ship which plied between Liverpool and Calcutta, and his wife Ann, after searching Liverpool for a suitable house, decided to purchase the commodious and comfortable residence at Number 20 Leveson Street. By the beginning of the following year, the Hinrichsons, together with their two sons, Henry George, aged five, and John Alfred, a three-year-old tot, and a maid-servant named Mary Parr, had settled into their new home. They found the place just a trifle large for their requirements and the Captain and his wife decided that it would be a good idea to let a couple of spare rooms which they had furnished but were not using. The money derived from such a source, together with what Mrs. Hinrichson earned by taking in a number of pupils to whom she taught music, would, they thought, help considerably towards household expenses.

Accordingly, a neat card was placed in the front parlour window announcing "Furnished Apartments to Let." Between three and four o'clock in the afternoon of the day when the notice was first exhibited, a well-dressed young man of about twenty-six years of age knocked at the door and asked in an engaging Irish brogue if he might inspect the rooms. He gave the name of John Gleeson Wilson, and said that he was a carpenter by trade and was employed by the Dock Estate. After being shown a front parlour and a back bedroom, Wilson expressed his entire satisfaction with the apartments, paid a week's rent in advance and took possession of the rooms there and then. That this was merely a subterfuge to gain entry to the house became apparent subsequently, for the man already had lodgings in another district of Liverpool.

Having handed over the money to Mrs. Hinrichson, Wilson left the house but returned at about eight o'clock that evening, when he retired to his room and, after sending out for a pint of ale at about ten, he went to bed.

Those were the days before "Dora" had come to put a curb upon the Englishman's drinking habits, and at half-past seven the following morning Wilson was in a public-house in Great George Street, having a breakfast glass of ale. Here, he did something which, in the light of later events, is utterly inexplicable. Calling the proprietress to his table, he asked her if she could supply him with a wafer with which to seal an envelope. The lady said that she did not happen to have one, but brought him a stick of sealing-wax with which he fastened down the flap. He then asked her if she would mind addressing the envelope for him as he was unable to write. The lady of the house summoned her daughter and she addressed the note "John Wilson, Esq., 20 Leveson Street, Liverpool," to his dictation.

Wilson then left the tavern and calling a youth whom he saw passing in the street, told him that if he would deliver a letter to a house to which he would direct him he would earn himself a few coppers. He instructed the lad to watch him into the house in Leveson Street and, when a few minutes had elapsed, to knock with the letter and ask whoever came to the door if John Wilson lived there, adding that he had a letter for him from his (Wilson's) employer.

The youth agreed to do this, and, after seeing Wilson disappear into the house, he proceeded, some five minutes later, to carry out his instructions.

The servant, Mary Parr, answered his knock.

"Does John Wilson live here?" he inquired.

"Yes, here he is," the girl replied as Wilson appeared behind her in the doorway. Borrowing some money from Mrs. Hinrichson to reward the boy, Wilson took the letter and returned to his room.

Shortly after eleven o'clock Mrs. Hinrichson called to Mary Parr that she was going out to do her shopping. She went first to a greengrocer's in nearby St. James's Street, where she was a regular customer, and ordered some potatoes. From there she went to a chandler's and bought two jugs. Both these purchases were to be sent to her house by errand-boys.

The boy with the vegetables arrived at Number 20 Leveson Street first. The door was opened by Wilson, who took the potatoes from him and returned a minute or two later with the empty basket. About twenty minutes afterwards the second boy arrived with the crockery. He put his basket down on the step . . . . rang the bell . . . whistled a popular tune while he waited . . . rang again . . . . . still no reply. Next he tried the effect of a thunderous assault on the knocker. The door remained tight shut. Putting his eye to the keyhole, the boy peeped into the hall, where he was startled to see a pair of woman's feet lying across the passageway. Overcome with curiosity, he climbed onto the handle of his basket and, perching himself precariously on the railings, peered in through the parlour window. What he saw in that room drained the colour from his face. The place was swimming with blood and lying there was the battered body of the maid servant; beside her, his head smashed to pulp, lay the five-year-old Henry. With a shriek of terror, the chandler's boy took to his heels, never stopping till he regained his father's shop. There, he stammered out his story and was sent helter-skelter in search of a policeman.

So it came about that the constable who was gently ambling along on his beat on that ordinary weekday afternoon, when all was so comfortingly quiet and peaceful about Duke Street, suddenly found himself involved in one of the most sensational Liverpool murder mysteries of the last century.

While the policeman and his young escort were making their way to Leveson Street, things were beginning to happen at that house of death. Scarcely had the chandler's boy fled the scene of horror, when a young lady who was a pupil of Mrs. Hinrichson's called for a music lesson. Receiving no reply to her repeated knockings, the girl became alarmed and, convinced that something was wrong, communicated her suspicions to a Mr. Hughes who was a neighbour of the Hinrichsons. This Mr. Hughes accompanied her to the house and, after looking through the parlour window and seeing the sight which had so unnerved the errand-boy, he broke a pane of glass and forced an entrance into the house.

So it was that when the police-officer and the lad arrived, they found the front door open and the house swarming with people. His scepticism blasted, the constable turned to the trembling boy: "Down to the bridewell as fast as you can go young 'un," he shouted, "and get them to send help quickly."

With the arrival of reinforcements, the police began a thorough search of the premises. They found attractive, 29-year-old Mrs. Hinrichson, who, by the way, was shortly expecting her third child, mortally injured in the lobby. Down in the cellar lay the three-year-old John, his throat cut from ear to ear. In the parlour was little Henry, also mortally wounded, and poor Mary Parr, who, though badly battered, was still just about alive. Upstairs in Wilson's room was a bowl of bloodstained water in which the murderer had evidently washed his hands, but of Wilson himself there was no sign.

In less than half an hour Mary Parr was in the Southern Hospital with anxious police officials watching beside her bed ready to take a statement should she regain consciousness. She did, briefly, and was able to falter out her story before, a few days later, she died.

Meanwhile, somewhere upon the high seas, Captain Hinrichson was sailing steadily towards home in his ship *Duncan*, blissfully unaware of the terrible blow which fate had struck to rob him of his entire family. Meanwhile, too, a human tiger prowled the drab jungle of the streets as the hunters set to work casting a drag-net to snare him.

Wilson's movements were decidedly odd. He went first to the Figure-of-Eight Pit in Toxteth Park, where he was seen washing his blood-smeared clothes. Next, he made his way to London Road and, after visiting a shop and offering a gold watch for sale, he went to a clothes dealer's in Great Homer Street where he bought a new pair of trousers. He also sold his boots to a poor woman and purchased another pair. After that, he returned to his original lodgings in Porter Street and asked his landlady for a clean shirt. She gave him one of her husband's and noticed that the one which he discarded was heavily stained.

At six o'clock on the evening of the murders, Wilson went to a barber's shop in Great Howard Street and had a shave. He asked the hairdresser if he could sell him a wig. Unable to do so, the man offered to take him to a shop in Oil Street where he could get one. On the way there, after questioning the barber as to the possibility of booking a passage to America for about £3, Wilson suddenly said: "Have you heard about the murder?" and upon the barber's replying that he had not, Wilson remarked: "A terrible affair, two women and two children had their heads bashed in."

"How awful! Did they get him?" asked his companion.

"No," replied Wilson, "not yet."

At that time Wilson had a wife living at Tranmere, and when he left the hairdresser he went over the water and spent the night with her.

Next morning, ignoring the hue and cry, he took a ferry-boat back to Liverpool and presented himself at the shop of Israel Samuel, a Great

Howard Street grocer who also dealt in watches. Wilson showed him a gold watch saying that he wanted £6 for it, but the grocer was not satisfied and before making an offer he called in a policeman. After examining the watch, the constable said he did not think it was one which had been notified as being stolen. Despite this reassurance, however, Samuel was still suspicious, and when the policeman had departed he said that he had not sufficient money on the premises to pay Wilson, but added that if he would accompany his son to his other shop in Dale Street he would be paid there. Before the pair left his shop, old Samuel told his son in Hebrew, "When you are passing the police-station, collar this fellow and give him in charge." The son did as his father told him and so surprised was Wilson that he had been bundled inside the bridewell before he could put up the slightest resistance.

Tried before Mr. Justice Patteson at the Liverpool Assizes, Wilson staunchly maintained his innocence. He showed no hint of remorse, refused to speak and while awaiting the verdict displayed "the most brutal indifference and ferocity of disposition." During the time he was in gaol he gave way to fits of uncontrollable rage and on one occasion nearly brained a warder with a hammer. His counsel argued that the evidence against him was wholly circumstantial, but the jury found "Guilty" without leaving the box. Their verdict was greeted with loud cheers by the huge crowds that had assembled outside the court-house.

Wilson, or, to give him his real name, Maurice Gleeson, who was a native of Limerick, was hanged on September 15th, 1849, outside Kirkdale Gaol in the presence of 30,000 spectators. Excursion trains, packed to suffocation, were run to the execution, and the Railway Companies advertised "Reduced fares for this occasion only."

On the scaffold, Wilson maintained a pose of stolid indifference and faced the crowd with lips curled in a contemptuous sneer. An eye-witness afterwards wrote: "A tremendous cheer went up from the vast multitudes when the dangling body of Gleeson Wilson swung from the gallows."

Ann Hinrichson, together with her unborn child, her two sons and Mary Parr, were all buried in the same grave in St. James's Cemetery. History is silent regarding what happened to Captain Hinrichson, apart from the fact that he subsequently gave up the sea and became dock master of Toxteth, Huskisson and finally Queen's Docks.

One last note. Leveson Street, which had become so notorious as a result of Wilson's dreadful deeds, was shortly afterwards re-named Grenville Street.

5. THE TWITCHING-FACE SLAYER

Back in the 'nineties, when the Liverpool waterfront was a spiky forest of masts and spars, old Edward Moyse was a familiar figure at the Pier Head, and until recently there were elderly folk who still remembered the little bookstall which he kept on Mann Island opposite George's Dock.

A picturesque character, with a straggling grey beard and a shock of flowing white hair, upon which was always perched a shabby top-hat, old Moyse was something of a recluse. He had few friends and lived alone in his home at Number 26 Redcross Street, except for 15-year-old John Needham, who helped him at his stall during the day and kept house for him after the shutters had been put up at the kiosk. Despite a certain eccentricity, Moyse seems to have been a good master and a man of markedly religious turn. You could see him every Sunday worshipping at St. Nicholas's Church, and his interest in affairs of the spirit extended even into the realms of his daily business, for, apart from dealing in newspapers, magazines and second-hand books, he made something of a speciality of selling bibles.

It was to this harmless old newsvendor that, on the night of February 18th-19th, 1895, death came in no gentle guise.

That evening the stall closed as usual at about 6 p.m., and John Needham went home alone to Redcross Street as his master had to go to view some books which he was proposing to purchase. Shortly after 6-30, young Needham, who was busying himself in preparing his supper, was startled by a loud knock at the door. Callers were few at that house, and he was surprised to find upon the doorstep a stranger who told him that he had come to buy some valuable books. The boy explained that Mr. Moyse was away from home and was not likely to be back before nine or ten o'clock that night. Upon hearing this, the man said that he would return at nine o'clock, but actually it was just striking eight when he came back, entering the house by means of a back-passage which he evidently knew well.

The stranger, who was subsequently identified as William Miller, a 27-year-old sailor, was obviously well acquainted with Moyse, but the exact nature of their relationship was at the time, and still is, shrouded in mystery. That there was some curious association between them, however, is beyond question.

When Miller appeared for the second time, Needham was engaged in making a pot of tea for himself. He offered the stranger a cup which he politely refused and, seating himself at the table, announced his intention of waiting until the bookseller arrived home. So, as the clock ticked on, these two sat peaceably chatting in the living-room, and the stranger confided that he was a seafarer. Evidently seeking to ingratiate himself with the lad, he promised that he would bring him home a parrot and some 'baccy from his very next voyage to foreign parts, and went on to say that he was due to be paid-off the following day, adding that Moyse's boys used frequently to go errands for him and were always right for two or three shillings. Changing the subject, Miller then made some remarks regarding Moyse's rather peculiar ways of walking and talking, but the lad did not take him up on this and was somewhat non-committal in his reply. For a while the conversation flagged until, suddenly, the sailor demanded:

"Where does the old chap keep his money?"

"I don't know," answered Needham.

But Miller was persistent, saying that he thought that the old man was very wealthy and asking Needham if he had never seen any of the cash which he had in the house.

"It's very funny that he doesn't tell you where his money is for fear he might die," commented Miller suspiciously.

But the boy only shook his head and said they didn't sell enough books to make a lot of money.

Apparently satisfied, Miller reverted to the topic of his impending pay-off, and told the youth that he wanted to give Mr. Moyse some sovereigns to keep for him, asking at the same time if he thought that his master would lend him sixpence till the morning. At that very moment, there was the sound of a key in the lock and Edward Moyse came in. That was at five minutes to ten.

The old man shook hands cordially with his visitor, saying as he did so that he had not expected to see him again so soon. Then, turning to Needham, he said, "This is the lodger I had before. He can sleep on the sofa tonight and you can make up the bed in the best bedroom for him tomorrow." The boy was then despatched upstairs to bed. With Needham's departure, the first scene of the drama came to an end. What transpired between the two men he left sitting amiably beside the living-room fire that night will never be known—only the fearful fate which was to overtake one of them, making front-page news next day and being remembered down the years as the terrible Redcross Street Murder.

It is at 5 a.m. on the morning of February 19th, 1895, that the curtain rises upon the second act of this real-life tragedy. Upstairs in his room below the eaves, John Needham stirs in his sleep as the nearby clock of St. Nicholas's chimes the hour. In the cold and dark of the winter morning, the boy struggles from his bed and lights a candle. He is not the only one abroad in that silent house. Presently, as he is pulling on his clothes, Miller comes into his bedroom. He is without his jacket and boots. He says that he cannot wake the master and that he is unable to find any coal with which to light a fire. The boy tells him that the coal is kept outside on the landing and that the coal-bucket and hatchet are on the floor below. Miller disappears downstairs. There is the clatter of a bucket, the sound of heavy treading, and a minute or two later he is back in Needham's bedroom. Standing in the doorway, he points to an aperture in the ceiling of the landing.

"What is that?" he asks.

"It is a manhole," replies Needham.

"Oh!" says Miller, "I must have a look up there," and with that fetches a chair, climbs onto it and pulls himself up through the trap. For fully ten minutes he is up there rooting about with his hands on the dusty floor. He does not, it seems, find what he is searching for, and, very quietly, Miller eases his way back through the trap-door and lowers himself to the landing. Stealthily, he creeps back into Needham's room, extinguishes the candle and deals the boy a vicious blow on the side of the head. Needham slumps onto the bed and, without a word, Miller falls upon him and grips him by the throat until he loses consciousness. When, a few minutes later, the lad regains his senses, he finds his assailant standing over him with a poker. He raises the weapon and brings it down with sickening force upon the youth's skull. Then he leaves the room and Needham, bleeding badly, dimly hears him call "Good morning," as he passes Mr. Moyse's bedroom. The front door opens, crashes to, and then there is silence. Needham lapses into unconsciousness.

Sometime later, he does not know how long for he has lost all sense of time, the injured boy manages to crawl to his master's room. There, he finds old Moyse dead in his bed, his head battered in, his silky white hair a matted tangle of congealed blood. Weak and dizzy from loss of blood and almost fainting with fright, Needham drags himself out into the street where he is found by a man who is walking through the sleeping town on his way to work. Soon, a little crowd of passers-by has gathered round the stricken boy and one of them identifies him as the youth who works for Edward Moyse. The police are summoned and young Needham is taken away in an ambulance to hospital.

While the doctors tended Needham's injuries, the police made their way to Redcross Street. There, they found a scene of ghastly confusion. The whole place had obviously been ransacked. There were signs of a severe struggle and the staircase was spattered with crimson sequins of blood. Upstairs, lay the battered corpse of Edward Moyse. The only money in the house was the sum of £8 which they discovered beneath Moyse's pillow. It did not take the police long to decide that this was no chance crime committed by a passing tramp, but the work of a local man who,

27

hearing tales of Moyse's miserly ways, had made up his mind to carry off his rumoured (but actually non-existent) crock of gold.

As soon as he was sufficiently recovered, Needham recounted the story of Miller's visit to the police, but when it came to giving a description of the man he began to realise how very little he really knew about him. That he was aged about twenty-five, dressed like a sailor and talked a great deal about the sea, was not much help in a port the size of Liverpool. But one of the officers happened to ask him if he had noticed anything peculiar about the fellow—strange tattoo marks or something really characteristic like that. The boy thought for a minute: yes, there *was* one thing: he had a queer way of twitching the right side of his face when excited.

That was more like it: here at last was something to go on, and this description was immediately circulated to every police-station in the North of England.

Time passed, and then one day a woman came to the police and told them that she knew the whereabouts of a man who she thought might be the murderer. He had a nervous twitch of the kind described and seemed loth to venture into the streets in daylight. His name was William Miller, he was a seaman, just back from America, and he was living with his father-in-law in Edgeware Street. A police cordon was thrown around the house. The wanted man was in bed and had no chance to get away. In his room they found a bloodstained shirt. Arrested, Miller protested his complete innocence. "My shirt got covered with blood at the Gill Street slaughterhouse where I had a job for a few days," he said. A reasonable explanation, or so it seemed, until he was taken to the slaughterhouse and told to point out the exact spot where he had been working when he got bloodstained. Without batting an eyelid, Miller said, "I was working just there," and went on to give a detailed account of the animals which had been killed there during his period of employment. They let him talk. When he had finished the superintendent of the abattoir said quietly: "We haven't killed any cattle in this part of the building for months past. Those carcases you now see were brought over from Birkenhead to be sold here."

The game was up. Miller surely knew as much, but he still tried to bluff his way out. So the police took him to the hospital; to the bedside of the boy he had tried to kill. At first Needham seemed rather doubtful as the police had brought a number of people with them, whom they lined up at the foot of his bed in the style of a regular identity parade. Outwardly calm, Miller must, however, have been inwardly agitated for, very slowly at first, the righthand side of his face BEGAN TO TWITCH. "Look at his face! Look at his face!" screamed the boy and dived in terror beneath the bedclothes. And, as the police-officers closed in upon him, William Miller, his face twitching ever more furiously, was led away to Walton and the gallows, a man whose face had betrayed him as surely as if he had been caught with the bloodstained poker in his hand.

6. THE GENTLE CHINAMAN

Almost sixty years after the hangman's noose has despatched him into the arms of his ancestors, the story of the tragedy that overtook Lock Ah Tam is still told in the Chinese quarter of Liverpool. It is a tale, too, that is whispered beneath the gay lanterns of far-away Tai-Ping, of Shanghai, Hong Kong and Singapore. What our bald speech debases to a matter of cold and senseless murder, is, doubtless, in the lilied tongue of the yellow men, elevated to the level of a parable. As they smoke their opium pipes, the oriental philosophers will find in the story of Lock Ah Tam a deep well of proverbial wisdom, and to the poor Chinaman it will seem to justify that wistful dubiety with which he is accustomed to regard wealth.

It was in the high summer of 1895 that 23-year-old Lock Ah Tam decided to abandon his berth as a ship's steward in favour of a clerk's desk in a Liverpool Shipping Office.

The move was to prove a wise one, for, possessed of a curiously charming personality, of honest and industrious habits and speaking fluent English, he advanced rapidly, until, in less than twenty-five years time, he had become a rich, respected and influential member of the community into which he had moved.

By 1918, Lock Ah Tam had to all outward appearances achieved a happy and well-balanced life. He lived in a delightful home in Birkenhead, which was presided over by his charming English wife, Catherine, who bore him a son Lock Ling, and two daughters, Doris and Cecilia, and had a host of friends whom he loved to entertain at his house.

And if the gods smiled upon him, Tam was not slow to appreciate their favour and he always tried to share his good fortune with those about him. He contributed most generously to local charities and could always be counted upon to extend a helping hand to anyone who was in trouble.

Indeed, he would go out of his way to discover deserving cases and his tenderness towards children was most marked. "I have seen him give half-crowns to little children when we have met them in the street," said one of his friends, "and then he has said 'Look at those poor people,' and we did not know them, and he would give them half-crowns."

Each Christmas he held a huge party at his own house, to which, irrespective of nationality, were invited a horde of the children of Liverpool's poor.

Tam's prestige and influence among Liverpool's Chinese community was immense, for the sympathetic nature of the man was such that he busied himself with all manner of social and political work for the benefit of his fellow-men, not only in the country of his adoption, but also in the

30

land of his birth.

Tam it was who became the European representative of what was virtually a Chinese seamen's trade union. Who but Tam should represent three important shipping lines in this country in all their negotiations with their Chinese employees? Tam was the man who was elected President of the greatest Republican Society in China, and the British agent of the cause of Sun Yat-Sen.

When the question arose of founding a club in Liverpool where Chinese sailors could meet their friends and enjoy a drink and a game of billiards in comfort and safety from land sharks, was it not Tam who, largely at his own expense, saw to it that that club was provided?

In a way it seems likely that it was this club of his which led to Tam's downfall.

One February evening in 1918, shortly before the Chinese New Year, Tam paid a visit to the club to have a drink and a game of billiards. It was while the game was in progress that the door suddenly burst open and the place was invaded by a gang of drunken Russian sailors. Tam ordered them to leave. They started to swear and shout and one of them, a little more drunk maybe than the others, seized a cue and dealt Tam a hefty blow on the head. He fell to the floor, bleeding profusely, but by the time the police arrived on the scene he was sufficiently recovered to walk to his office in the house next door. And later in the night he was able to spend an hour at the police-station and accompany the officers to a nearby lodging-house in order to identify the man who had attacked him.

Nevertheless, it seems that the damage resulting from that chance-struck blow was considerably greater than at first appeared, for thereafter the whole of Tam's character underwent a most distressing change. From being, as we have seen, a kindly, acute and lovable man, he became irritable, absent-minded and morose. Always a moderate drinker, he took to the bottle with a vengeance. Previously, he had confined himself pretty well to whisky, of which he could carry a very considerable cargo. Up to the time of his injury no one had ever seen him drunk, and he always attributed its lack of unfortunate effect upon him to the fact that to every glass of whisky it was his custom to add two teaspoonfuls of salt. Now, however, he started to mix his drinks and tottered upon the brink of chronic alcoholism.

He began, too, to display sudden uncontrollable bursts of maniacal temper on the slightest—real or imagined—provocation. He would flare-up in an instant, stamp his feet, foam at the mouth and his bloodshot eyes would bulge out from his purple, swollen face like those of a madman. The most trivial thing could send him off into one of those paroxysms.

31

On one occasion, for example, Tam was entertaining seven or eight friends to supper at his house. One of them, a Mr. Jones, who had been his close associate for many years, made some completely innocuous remark. The effect on Tam was terrifying. He sprang to his feet, his face distorted with rage, foaming at the mouth, gabbling and waving his arms about like one demented. Seizing all the glasses on the table, he hurled them one after the other into the fireplace before collapsing, exhausted, into his chair.

Again, one evening Tam invited a taxi-driver into his house for a drink. Thinking to please his generous fare, the driver made some flattering reference to China, whereupon Tam instantly flew into another of his celebrated rages.

In 1922, Tam invested more than £10,000 in a shipping venture. It failed and he lost every penny that he had put into it. Moreover, his business in Liverpool had ceased to prosper and in 1924 he was made bankrupt. The crowning tragedy of Tam's career came on November 31st, 1925. It was his son Lock Ling's twentieth birthday. The boy had only recently returned to Liverpool after nine years absence in China. It was, therefore, an occasion of much rejoicing and Tam was giving a select little dinner-party. Happily, all went well. Tam remained sober and when the last guest had departed at a quarter to one in the morning no untoward incident had sullied the festive pleasantry of the proceedings. About twenty minutes after the household had retired to bed, Lock Ling was distressed to hear stampings, shufflings and shoutings coming from his parents' bedroom. Promptly concluding that his father was ill-treating his mother, he got out of bed and, accompanied by his two sisters, went to her aid. He accused Tam of hitting his mother, an accusation which Tam indignantly refuted. There was a noisy scene and Lock Ling threatened to take his mother next door to spend the rest of the night with Mr. and Mrs. Chin.

Lock Ling, Mrs. Lock, Doris and Cecilia then all went into the sitting-room and Lock Ling said that he was going to get Mr. Chin and begged his mother and sisters to go with him. But Mrs. Lock refused. So he went off on his own.

Apart from the Locks, there lived in the house a young woman named Margaret Sing who had for five or six years acted as companion to Mrs. Lock. Throughout the trouble Margaret Sing had remained quietly in her room. Now, she heard Tam shouting her name. She went out onto the landing and he told her to bring him his boots. She did so and Tam ordered her to get dressed. Presently, fully dressed, she returned to her employer's bedroom. She found the door ajar and peeping inside she caught a glimpse of Tam's face reflected in a mirror. It was a twisted mask of fury and in his hand he held a revolver.

Silently, Margaret Sing tiptoed to the sitting-room, and told the three women what she had just seen. Swiftly they closed and barricaded the door. It was not a second too soon, for barely had they done so than Tam began battering upon it and screaming that he must be let in. After a few minutes he stopped, and the listening women heard him go back to his room. Very softly they opened the door and crept, trembling, down to the kitchen.

There they found Lock Ling and Mrs. Chin. Hearing what had just happened upstairs, Lock Ling again begged his mother to take his sisters and Margaret Sing to the safety of the next door house. Still Mrs. Lock refused to do so, and the desperate boy ran off in search of a policeman.

The women stood round the kitchen table whispering for a while until Margaret Sing took some crockery into the scullery. The others followed her. The scullery was small and there was not room for them all. Margaret stood together with Mrs. Chin and Doris behind the widely open door. Cecilia was by the gas-stove and Mrs. Lock remained standing in the doorway.

All at once there was a deafening report and Tam's wife crumpled up on the floor. Then the wicked-looking barrel of a gun slid round the doorway and there was a second ear-splitting explosion. This time Cecilia slumped to the ground and Tam came swiftly and silently into the scullery. Spittle bubbled and trickled from his mouth; he had a revolver in one hand and a rifle in the other. He raised the revolver and shot Doris.

Leaving the three women on the scullery floor, Tam then walked to the telephone, lifted the receiver and said: "I have shot my wife and children. Please put me on to the Town Hall."

The operator put him through to Birkenhead Central Police-Station: "Send your folks, please. I have killed my wife and children," was all he said.

At his trial, which opened on February 5th, 1926, before Mr. Justice MacKinnon, Tam was defended by Sir Edward Marshall Hall, who claimed that his client had not been responsible for his crime, but had committed it while in a state of epileptic automatism.

Said that great advocate, it was directly due to the injury which he had received in 1918 that the prisoner had committed his crime, for that injury had lead to the gradual deterioration of the man's intellectual and moral character, to a craving for alcohol and to epilepsy.

It took the jury precisely twelve minutes to find Tam guilty.

As the judge passed the death sentence the sound of continuous sobbing filled the court which was crowded with Tam's friends. Only Lock Ah Tam remained calm. He stood there erect in the dock, the faint line of a smile upon his heavy features. Maybe at the end some deep oriental instinct for philosophy had come to his aid. Maybe his mind was far away from that gloomy, panelled courtroom back amid the smiling lotus blossoms of his sun-lit native land.

7. THE BARBAROUS SEA-CAPTAIN

If ever Captain Bligh of the *Bounty* had a rival, it must surely have been Captain Henry Rogers, master of the *Martha and Jane*, whose ferocious and brutal treatment of an unfortunate seaman named Andrew Rose was to lead him to a dry dock somewhat different from those to which he had grown accustomed in the course of his maritime life—that of the Crown Court in St. George's Hall, Liverpool, where, on an August day in 1857, he stood at the bar to answer a charge of Murder on the High Seas.

It was towards the end of April 1857, that Rogers and Rose joined the barque *Martha and Jane*, then lying off the Barbados, the one as captain and the other as a lowly member of the crew. Rogers, who took command of the vessel, was thirty-seven years old. A native of Aberdeen, he had spent twenty-three years at sea and had earned a reputation as a reliable master. Rose, on the other hand, was "an amiable, quiet man who would harm no one, but a little weak in the head." He claimed that he had had more than twenty years experience of the sea and was signed on as an able seaman. As a matter of fact he seems to have been anything but able. Almost as soon as he came aboard, Rose was put to work by Charles Seymour, the second mate, and such a hash did he make of the job that the mate beat him most severely. Indeed, so savage was the beating that Rose's fellow crew-members advised him to run away. He did so, but was caught and brought back by the police on May 10th. Rose was immediately put in irons and on May 11th the *Martha and Jane* weighed anchor and set sail for Liverpool.

Then began an orgy of senseless cruelty which it is terrible to contemplate.

On May 12th Rose was thrashed by Captain Rogers, William Miles (the first mate), and Seymour; and thereafter never a day passed but he was kicked and flogged with a rope-end or whip. In the end, the floggings seem to have lost all meaning or relation to events, a sort of blood lust took hold of the Captain and his unsavoury mates and at any hour of the day or night when they felt so inclined they would pitch into the luckless Rose.

One Sunday morning when the voice of Rose, who had a fondness for singing, was heard raising itself piously to the heavens in the Primitive Methodist hymn "O Let Us be Joyful," the effect on Rogers was extraordinary. He descended, cursing, to where Rose lay in irons trying to be joyful, and shouted, "I'll make you sorrowful." He then ordered the mate to fetch a large iron bolt. This he forced into Rose's mouth, the mates tying it in with yarn. The bolt was left in the choking man's mouth for an hour and a half.

35

As the voyage wore on, the Captain introduced further refinements into his blackguardly treatment of Rose. He had on board a dog which he used to set on him with the command, "Bite that man." The dog entered into the spirit of the thing and eventually whenever Rogers came forward with his whip the dog would automatically fly at Rose and savage him, tearing great pieces of flesh from his legs, thighs and arms.

His body became black and blue all over and covered with dozens of festering wounds, running sores and ulcers.

By way of infusing a little variety into the proceedings, he would sometimes be sent aloft naked to furl the sail, the mate following him up the mast with a whip, lashing him until the blood spurted from his body. For several days he was kept entirely without clothing, exposed to the cold sea-winds and finding what cover he could at night. On yet another occasion, in order to "cure him of his filthy habits," Captain Rogers forced Rose to eat his own excrement and plugged his nostrils with it.

Then, the Captain dreamed up another little torture. He knocked the end out of a water-cask, forced the hapless Rose into it, headed it up again and spent a few merry hours rolling it up and down the deck. Finally, he had it lashed to the side of the ship and Rose, cramped, stifling and with only the bung-hole to breathe through, was kept there for twelve hours. Some of the crew, taking pity on him, gave Rose a little pea-soup and some water, but one of the mates, discovering this concession to ordinary humanity, became so furious that they dared not interfere again.

It was when the *Martha and Jane* was seven days out from Liverpool that the final act of cruelty was perpetrated. After all he had endured, it is hardly to be wondered at that when the Captain said roughly, "Rose, I wish you would either drown or hang yourself," the man answered in despair, "I wish you would do it for me." Hearing this, Rogers and the two mates seized Rose and led him to the mainmast. They got a rope, made a timber-hitch in it, slipped the noose round his neck and hoisted him up.

For fully two minutes Rose remained suspended by his neck a couple of feet above the deck. His face turned black, his eyes and tongue protruded and he began to froth at the mouth, and when at length he was let down he fell flat upon the deck and lay there like one dead. The Captain was heard to say to one of the crew that if he had been kept hanging half a minute longer he would have been finished.

After that the crew managed to get Rose down to the fo'castle, but he had become unhinged by all he had undergone and was so crazed that they were obliged to tie his hands. He remained in the crew's quarters a day or two and on the morning of June 5th, he was taken up on deck again in order that he might wash himself. By this time, however, he was so weak that he could scarcely crawl and he lay upon the deck with his head towards the forward hatch and the water washing over his legs. And there, some hours later, he died. Such was the state of his body, a festering mass of evil-smelling and maggot-infested wounds, that the crew were loth to touch it. They dragged him aft with a rope and by the Captain's order the corpse was thrown overboard.

When, on June 9th, the *Martha and Jane* arrived at Liverpool, information was laid by the crew and the Captain and the first and second mates were arrested.

Captain Rogers on being taken into custody said that he had almost expected it for he had heard "that villain Groves" (a seaman on board and one of the principal witnesses for the prosecution) wanted to get up something of the kind against him in order that he might get ten shillings a day for attending the police-court.

He further alleged that he had seen Groves ill-use Rose and said that when he first came aboard Rose was covered with sores as a result of sleeping out in the fields in Barbados. He also stated that he himself had never done Rose the slightest harm apart from whipping him for being dirty.

The trial of Henry Rogers, William Miles and Charles Edward Seymour took place at St. George's Hall on August 19th, 1857, and when the jury announced a verdict of guilty the court was startled by a succession of loud cheers from the crowd which was assembled in the large hall outside. All three were sentenced to death but a recommendation to mercy was acted upon in the cases of the two mates, who were subsequently reprieved.

During the time he spent in Kirkdale Gaol an amazing change came over the barbarous sea-captain—a transformation which, it must be remarked, takes place extraordinarily frequently in the cases of cornered bullies and captured murderers. He turned wholeheartedly to the consolations of religion. He began to lament the neglect of his religious duties in early life and there was a touching little scene when, before taking his final leave of his two mates, he insisted upon praying with them and bestowed upon them the benefits of a great deal of pious and kindly advice. Indeed, his demeanour was such that, when it was all over, the chaplain volunteered: "He has been in the constant habit of praying, even when I have not been with him, very beautifully and very fervently and in a most delightful manner, which gave me much pleasure."

In the circumstances, one feels that the good padre was just a trifle carried away when he added: "He had a very feeling heart." And although Mr. Wright (the prison philanthropist) claimed: "I never met one more so," one has the distinct impression that Andrew Rose might have ventured to disagree with their pronouncements!

On the morning of his execution—September 12th, 1857—Captain Rogers, after bidding farewell to his wife and five children, who had come up from their home in Swansea in order to be near him, remained in the prison chapel engaged in religious exercises until a few minutes before twelve noon. Outside the gaol milled a great crowd, twenty or thirty thousand strong, of thieves, prostitutes, vagabonds, the residents of vile courts and cellars, such as were invariably attracted to the scenes of public executions. The women were for the main part disreputable and abandoned characters who "seemed by their conversation and manner highly delighted at having an opportunity of seeing a man hanged." But apart from the usual assemblage of human riff-raff, there could be seen, not only many in the unmistakable dress of the common seaman, but also a number of those holding higher positions—such as ships' captains and mates. According to Mr. Wright, the aforesaid philanthropist, Captain Rogers was "sadly frightened of facing the crowd," and before walking out to the scaffold expressed his deep obligation to the chaplain and the governor for their kind and charitable feelings and also to all the prison officers, adding, somewhat incongruously all things considered, that if he lived for a thousand years he should not forget their kindness!

The mood of the crowd may be gauged from the remark of a sailor who, looking up at the gallows, said with a leer. "My word, he'll be a different man on *that* quarter-deck than he was on the quarter-deck on the *Martha and Jane*. He will look more like a cook than a captain." This last referred to the white cap which is pulled over the eyes of the hangman's victim.

When, shortly after twelve o'clock, Captain Rogers appeared on the platform, he carried himself with great courage and dignity and, until the white cap covered his face, he stood gazing over the sea of heads below him, across the city to where the ships were riding the Mersey. In a matter of minutes, Mr. Hangman Calcraft had despatched him and Able Seaman Rose was avenged.

Within four days of his death, a model of Captain Rogers was on display in the Chamber of Horrors of Mr. Alsopp's Crystal Palace Waxworks in Lime Street. The waxen effigy, 5 feet 7 inches in height, was that of a stoutish, handsome, florid man, with sandy hair and light blue eyes set in a long face, to which a sharp nose and the absence of one of the upper teeth lent a slightly sinister aspect. Clad in the actual clothes which he had been wearing when he was executed—which Alsopp had purchased from Calcraft—the likeness was said to be first-rate and for many, many years it remained one of the greatest bogeys in the waxworks. But time, which alters all things, brought about the closure of both Mr. Alsopp's and nearby Reynold's waxworks, where the Captain had also a place of horripilatory honour, and the memory of his dark doings and the price he paid for them passed away.

To this day, however, you will still hear bated talk among the rapidly thinning ranks of old sailormen of the barbarous sea-captain whose terrible history is here set forth, and the record of whose deeds is perhaps the greatest blot on Liverpool's brave history of they who go down to the sea in ships.

8. THE BORGIA SISTERS OF THE LIVERPOOL SLUMS

The hearse, together with the line of empty mourning coaches, stood, that grey October afternoon more than a hundred years ago, forlornly in the roadway outside the house in Ascot Street.

Inside, behind the drawn blinds, a group of middle-aged women in rusty black dresses was clustered about a coffin in which lay the body of the husband of one of them, and the clinking of glasses, mingled with the plangency of drunken laughter, sounded unpleasantly irreverent in that tiny room of death. There was not, you might think, much of grief there.

The grisly party was reaching its climax when suddenly, without a word of warning, three men entered the house. As if by magic, the noise stopped. With a little cry of fear, one of the women bolted for the back-door and fled up the alley.

"I am the coroner's officer," said a quiet voice, "and these two gentlemen are doctors. I have an Order to stop the funeral. Which of you is Mrs. Higgins?"

Margaret Higgins stepped tremulously forward.

"The dead man Thomas Higgins was your husband?"

"Yes."

"Well, I'm afraid the burial won't be able to take place today, Mrs. Higgins; there's going to have to be a post-mortem."

There's going to have to be a post-mortem! Those eight words sealed the fate of 44-year-old Margaret Higgins, a charwoman, and her 54-year-old sister Catherine Flannagan, described as a lodging-house keeper, as surely as those other eight words which were to be pronounced by Mr. Justice Brett just four months later—"Hanged by the neck until you are dead."

The game was up and they both knew it. It was only a matter of time now before the doctors would discover those tell-tale red patches on the stomach, and the chemists recover the death-dealing powder of arsenic from the viscera, of the late Mr. Thomas Higgins.

The story of the crimes of Margaret Higgins and Catherine Flannagan, those two ruthless poisoners of the Liverpool slums, is a sordid one. There is nothing of grandeur about it. All that they did was mean and petty. It was murder most mercenary, and no less than four innocent people lost their lives to sate an overwhelming greed.

The commencement of this cold-blooded partnership in crime dates back to the year 1880. At that time Mrs. Flannagan and her sister were occupying a house in Skirving Street. Both were widows, women of drunken and morally dubious character, and they shared the house with five other people—John Flannagan, the Widow Flannagan's 22-year-old son; Thomas Higgins, a lodger, who was later to commit the grave indiscretion of marrying Margaret Higgins; Mary Higgins, the aforesaid Thomas Higgins's 8-year-old daughter; another lodger named Patrick Jennings, who was a dock labourer, and Jennings's 16-year-old daughter, Margaret.

The first of the many deaths which were to decimate this household of seven occurred in the December of 1880, when John Flannagan died and his grieving mother lost no time in collecting the £71 8s. for which he was insured with no less than five societies.

Towards the end of the following year, Margaret took Thomas Higgins, the lodger, who was a bricklayer's labourer, for her second husband (her first had been a Mr. Thompson) and in the November of 1882 little Mary Higgins died and her stepmother made haste to draw the £22 10s. club money.

Two months later Margaret Jennings was dead. She, too, had been heavily insured, and a couple of days after the unfortunate girl's death Mrs. Flannagan claimed the insurance money.

Thus far, three people had died within the space of two years and two months. No awkward questions had been asked and a reasonable profit had been forthcoming, but you couldn't go on having people die in your house without the neighbours starting to talk. For a time you might succeed in countering wagging tongues by actually prophesying the death of your victim from the time you had marked him down. Mrs. Flannagan had done that in John's case. "My son is very ill," she had said to a neighbour, "he's in consumption and will go off like all the other cases. He will never live to comb a grey hair." And when he obligingly fulfilled her gloomy forebodings no one was a whit surprised.

Again, it was not policy to strike when your intended was in the best of health. Far better to be patient and wait until some trifling ailment provided the opportunity to administer, under the guise of devoted nursing, the fatal dose. That way you also had less difficulty in getting the doctor, who had been attending the invalid anyway, to issue a death certificate. Still, three deaths in one house were enough however you looked at it, and so the ghoulish sisters and the two remaining members of their ménage removed to 105 Latimer Street.

They remained there until the following September and, strange to relate, there were no further deaths. In September, however, when the household removed once more, this time to 27 Ascot Street, a fresh victim was selected in the person of Thomas Higgins and the Borgia-like sisters made careful plans to ensure that their fourth killing should prove worthwhile. Mr. Higgins had policies effected on him to the tune of nearly

£100. An attempt to secure a further policy for £50 was made by Mrs. Flannagan, but the company in question insisted that any person insured for such a sum should undergo a medical examination. An agent, accompanied by a doctor, called on Thomas Higgins and their reception by that worthy, who happened to be drunk and had in any case heard nothing of the matter, was not exactly friendly. Actually, it was this final piece of greed which was to prove the women's undoing, for when, on October 2nd, 1883, Thomas Higgins died, of what his doctor certified as dysentery due to excessive drinking, it was his brother Patrick who, having in all probability heard from Thomas of this unsuccessful attempt to insure his life, began, on the day after his death, to make certain inquiries.

He visited a number of insurance societies and found that the life of his deceased brother had been insured with several of them and that the money had been already drawn. He went also to see the doctor who had attended Thomas Higgins, told him of his suspicions and together they approached the coroner, with the result that the funeral was stopped, a post-mortem ordered, the arsenic in Thomas Higgins's corpse discovered and Mrs. Higgins arrested.

Mrs. Flannagan, the woman who had fled from the house in Ascot Street, was arrested a few days later. She had been moving from one lodging-house to another but was finally cornered through the information of a woman who took pity on her and whilst entertaining her to tea suddenly recognised her as the person for whom the police were searching.

On October 16th both sisters were formally charged with murder. With the two women safely under lock and key, the police set to work to build up the case against them. The house in Ascot Street was searched and a flask-shaped bottle containing a turbid whitish fluid, a mug and a spoon were found. There was also a "market pocket" which Mrs. Higgins had been wearing at the time of her arrest. The liquid and the pocket both contained traces of arsenic. The bodies of Margaret Jennings, Mary Higgins and John Flannagan were all exhumed and in each case the remains of fatal doses of arsenic were recovered.

It subsequently became apparent that Mrs. Flannagan had really been the leading spirit in the macabre partnership, but she did her best to foist the blame onto her younger sister and actually offered to turn Queen's evidence in order to save her own neck. The offer was refused.

The trial, which opened at St. George's Hall on February 14th, 1884, lasted three days, and after an absence of forty minutes the jury returned with a verdict of guilty against both prisoners. Catherine Flannagan listened to the words of the death sentence unmoved: in the dock beside her her sister was practically prostrated.

When three clear Sundays had elapsed they were hanged. It was on the morning of March 3rd, 1884, and it was in a snowstorm, that the two Irish sisters, to whom must go the credit for having invented the method (adopted without acknowledgement by Mrs. Maybrick just five years later!) of obtaining arsenic by soaking fly-papers in water, paid, as it were, the patenting fees upon their murderous invention in the execution shed of old Kirkdale Gaol.

9. WHO WAS HANNAH BRADE?

Here and there in out-of-the-way corners of Liverpool there linger, like islands marooned by the tide of time, quiet, brooding squares of old-fashioned houses.

Such houses have, as the saying has it, come down in the world, but in the curve of a cracked fanlight and the curlicued elegance of a wrought-iron railing it is still possible to descry something of their former glories.

What lifetimes of triumph and tragedy have been lived beyond the peeling paintwork of their pillared porticos? What multitudes of strange stories have reached their climax and their close within their foursquare walls?

One at least of these real-life legends, which clings about the crumbling brickwork of such a house within a stone's throw of busy Islington Square, has been preserved, and it makes as strange reading as anything that the pages of the past can furnish.

About the year 1830, a widow who lived with her only daughter and young son in this particular house was seeking a maid-servant. Upon the recommendation of another respectable widow woman who kept a small-ware shop in London Road, a young woman who gave the name of Hannah Brade applied for the situation and was duly enagaged.

The girl arrived at the widow's house very shabbily attired and with her hair most dowdily coiffured in what was a somewhat obvious attempt to disguise the really outstanding refinement and loveliness of her face.

She was to remain in that lady's service for close on two years, and in the course of that time a number of curious characteristics of a type which might not ordinarily have been expected in a serving-maid of the period were noticed by her mistress.

Not that there was anything peculiar to remark in the way in which she carried out her duties—unless it was that she seemed more than usually careful and conscientious—and her manner was always grave, humble and reserved. But her mistress quickly observed that whenever people whom she did not know were coming to the house Hannah became inexplicably timid and uneasy. This unease rapidly disappeared, however, once she had made their acquaintance. It almost seemed as if she had been terrified in case they recognised her and as soon as she was assured that they did not, her normal happy demeanour reasserted itself. In all other respects Hannah was far from being timorous, and on once occasion when she was alone in the house she put two powerful villains who had come to burgle the place to flight. Moreover, for all the care she took to hide her light under the bushel of her anonymity, those whom she served soon discovered that she was possessed of a considerable knowledge of medicine and the treatment of the sick and saw her fearlessly and most efficiently tend a case of severe and disfiguring contagious disease.

On one or two totally unpremeditated occasions the mask slipped and she was proved to be thoroughly proficient in several foreign languages. Again, the chance discovery of a beautiful drawing revealed the fact that Hannah was no novice with a pencil. Indeed, this strange young lady's accomplishments were legion and far outdistanced the kitchen in their scope. One day when the family had been away from home they were both mystified and enchanted to hear the lovely liquid notes of a Beethoven sonata cascading from the window. Of course it was Hannah, who, thinking herself safe from observation, had crept quietly into the drawing-room and, seating herself at the piano, had abandoned herself to the rare delight of playing, with exquisite touch, a repertoire of music which she loved.

Then one morning they found Hannah's little room amid the eaves abandoned. The girl had gone as mysteriously as she came. For fully two months there was no word of her. But Hannah had not forgotten her late employer, for at the end of that time a package was delivered to the house and in its tissue-papered depths they found a selection of most costly gifts addressed to all who had shown kindness to the vanished girl.

And after that there was never another word or sign, but for many, many years afterwards it was a common question to ask in Liverpool: "Who was Hannah Brade?"

No one has ever been able to supply the answer.

Now, more than a century and a half has gone by since Hannah disappeared and we are still no nearer to the truth. Maybe, somewhere in this vast city there is one person who, brushing aside the cobwebbed shroud the years have woven about it, could reveal a long-guarded family secret that would dispel this time-honoured mystery. Maybe, however, it is not a pretty story, a tale of love, or the want of it, that is best forgotten. All that we need to know is that, whatever the reason, it drove a beautiful and refined young girl to take brief shelter behind a serving-wench's apron.

10. CORPSE IN THE PARLOUR

Although murder is always horrible, there are some circumstances in which the horror which it provokes is subject to a subtle heightening. For instance, the corpse in the library of the ancient manor-house seems somehow far less out of place than the battered body in the front parlour of the surburban villa. Likewise, murder is always more terrible when it involves average men and women in an everyday setting: one gets the uncomfortable feeling that it could so easily have been oneself.

The matter of murder which is to come under consideration here is one of the great criminological puzzles of all time and has already been used as the basis for no less than three detective novels.*

There is nothing to distinguish Anfield's Wolverton Street from any other of a hundred just such streets of neat, red-brick terrace houses which lie about the perimeter of our city. It is not a mean street, nor for that matter is it a particularly prosperous one. It might, perhaps, be best described as an "ordinary street"; and there, in essence you have the horror, for it was to this "ordinary street," upon a dark January evening in the year 1931, that tragedy came, leaving a bloodstained visiting-card at Number 29—the home of Mr. and Mrs. William Herbert Wallace.

The story of the murder of Julia Wallace may be said to begin in the early evening of the day immediately preceding that upon which the actual crime was committed. At the point where Breck Road meets Priory Road there stands a telephone box, and shortly after seven o'clock on the evening of January 19th, 1931, a shadowy figure might have been seen occupying its red-framed interior. In the nearby telephone exchange a signal flashed a call from Anfield 1627. There is some discussion. A man's voice rasps along the wire; "Operator, I have pressed button 'A,' but have not had my correspondent yet." The caller is connected with Bank 3581. It is a small incident, a daily occurrence, but it has to be recorded. The operator forgets it: but with the ringing of the telephone it is as if the call-bell for the first act of a tragedy is heard, summoning the actors to the stage. And the bell sounds its echo in the City Café in North John Street, where it is answered by a waitress. She does not yet know it, but she is about to speak to a murderer. His strong, metallic voice asks for Mr. Wallace. She knows that Wallace is a member of the Liverpool Central Chess Club which holds its meetings in this café. A glance tells her that he is not in the room, however, so she calls a Mr. Samuel Beattie, who is captain of the Chess Club, to the telephone.

*The Jury Disagree by George Goodchild & Bechofer Roberts (Jarrolds, 1934).
 Skin for Skin by Winifred Duke (Gollancz, 1935).
 The Telephone Call by John Rhode (Bles, 1948).

Later that evening Beattie tells Wallace that a man named Qualtrough has rung up and wants to see him on business at 25 Menlove Gardens East, at seven-thirty p.m. on the morrow. Qualtrough had regretted that he would be unable to ring back later, as he was busy celebrating his daughter's twenty-first birthday. That, Beattie conjectured, might have something to do with the business matter which he wanted to discuss with Wallace, who was an agent of the Prudential Assurance Company. Wallace seemed puzzled, and several times expressed his ignorance as to the identity of Qualtrough and the location of Menlove Gardens East. Nevertheless, he made a careful entry in his notebook before resuming his interrupted game of chess.

That night, as they sat quietly in their little back kitchen, Wallace doubtless discussed the matter with his wife. The arrangement was vague, even mysterious, but a root-deep instinct whispered the promise of business—good business, perhaps. A daughter's twenty-first birthday party—that might mean a £100 endowment policy, and at twenty per cent. commission on the first payment, well, to fishers in small pools the prospect of such a catch would certainly have appeared irresistible.

There is nothing about the early part of Tuesday, January 20th, to indicate that it was a day in any way different from any other day in the normal routine of an insurance agent's wife. Wallace did his usual round of collecting and returned home at about five past six in the evening. After tea, apparently determined to cast an optimistic net, he gathered together a selection of those forms which he thought appropriate to the type of business which he hoped to transact, went upstairs, washed, brushed his hair and put on a clean collar. Surveying himself in the mirror, he must have seen with some satisfaction the image of a man, neatly attired and carefully toileted; a man conscientiously patterned to create a favourable impression upon a prospective client.

According to his own account, it was about a quarter to seven when Wallace left the house. He went out by the back-door and made his way down the cobbled entry, which runs behind Wolverton Street, towards the tram stop. Walking down the alley, tall, thin and neat, Wallace becomes for us a figure of enigma. There is nothing in the appearance of this man, who is so soon to step from the respectable shadows of a quiet life into the brief, black limelight of the dock, to suggest that it is a different Wallace who treads a familiar way—a Wallace who has become a murderer. Yet, that is the problem for us to ponder. Is this a callous murderer setting forth through the night to establish a cunningly-contrived alibi, or an innocent man, unhappily victim of a deeply-woven plot?

The precise hour of Wallace's departure from his house cannot be fixed, but there can be no doubt of the fact that round about ten past seven he was boarding a tram at the junction of Lodge Lane and Smithdown Road, a point which was a good twenty minutes journey from his home.

From this time onwards, Wallace is never lost sight of for very long. There are tram conductors who are able to testify to his fussy progress as far as Menlove Avenue. A clerk, whom he stopped in the street, the householder's wife at 25 Menlove Gardens West, a policeman, whom he met in Green Lane, and the manageress of Allday's newsagent's shop in Allerton Road, are all able to bear witness to Wallace's hunt for the elusive Qualtrough and the non-existent Menlove Gardens East. Weary at last of his unsuccessful searchings, Wallace decided to give up his quest and head homewards.

It was at about eight forty-five that Mr. and Mrs. John Sharp Johnston, who lived at 31 Wolverton Street, chancing to emerge into the alley behind their house, saw Wallace walking towards his own back-gate. To their amiable "Good evening", he replied with the strange-seeming question, "Have you heard anything at all unusual going on tonight?" He explained that he could not get into his house, having found both front and back doors barred against him. The Johnstons watched while he tried once again to open the back-door. This time his efforts met with success. "It opens now," he said, in surprised tones. Wallace disappeared inside. His good neighbours waited outside, just to see that all was well. They heard him call his wife; they saw the flaring-up of gas-jets that betokened his progess through the dark house. Then, suddenly, a tense, white-faced Wallace came rushing out into the yard. "Come and see—she has been killed!" he gasped.

In the front parlour, close to the fireplace, lay the huddled corpse of Julia Wallace. It needed no pathologist to see that murder had been done. The dead woman's skull had been smashed like an egg, and the repeated blows of a frenzied attack had spilled its yoke of brains upon the floor. Everywhere was blood; the sedate sitting-room had become a slaughterhouse, and all about, the dull, red flush of bloodstains sullied familiar surfaces with ugly, alien patterns.

During the next few nightmare hours, that small, undistinguished house became the focus of an unaccustomed attention. Police and men of medicine made extensive examinations. But for all their skill, they could deduce nothing beyond the fact that a woman had been brutally done to death in a house which exhibited no signs of having been broken into. And for all their searchings, they could discover no single significant trace of blood outside the confines of that blood-drenched parlour. Despite the fact that nothing but the happiest of relationships could be shown to have existed between Wallace and his wife, suspicion crystallized into accusation, and, on purely circumstantial evidence, Wallace was, on February 2nd, arrested and taken to Walton Gaol.

From the windows of the prison hospital he saw the barren trees put on their scanty green coats, and watched the first few flowers poke modest heads between the asphalt cracks. For him, the young sun's pallid promise of summer meant very little, for in his heart he knew that he might never live to see its fulfilment.

His trial opened at the Liverpool Spring Assizes on April 22nd, 1931, before Mr. Justice Wright. It was not long before the line which the Crown intended to take became obvious. The prosecution alleged that on the evening of January 19th, Wallace had telephoned to the City Café, and, in the character of Qualtrough, had left the message for himself. On the following evening he had murdered his wife, avoiding contamination by bloodstains by committing the crime either in the nude, or clad only in an old mackintosh (a mackintosh had been found tucked beneath Julia Wallace's body). By the time Mr. Hemmerde, the Crown Counsel, sat down, the case against Wallace certainly looked very black.

But Mr. Roland Oliver did not seem unduly perturbed as he rose to open for the defence. He suggested that the crime was the work of an unknown enemy of the Wallaces, who had waited in the vicinity of Wolverton Street to make sure that Wallace was not going to be in the City Café when he rang up with his bogus message. It might be that Wallace would recognize his voice. Passing then to the night of the crime, Oliver was able to produce witnesses who stated that Mrs. Wallace had been seen alive as late as six forty-five. It was, he argued, inconceivable that the prisoner could have committed the crime and washed and dressed himself all in a matter of five, or at the most ten, minutes, as he would have to have done if he was to be at Lodge Lane at seven-ten, a fact which was not disputed by the prosecution.

The medical witnesses stated that the murderer was bound to be extensively stained by his victim's blood. Careful examination had revealed neither damp towels nor any signs of a bath having been taken at Wolverton Street, nor did any of Wallace's clothes bear any traces of blood. Oliver was careful to stress the fact that no motive whatsoever had been adduced, and no weapon had been discovered. After an hour's absence, the jury returned a verdict of Guilty.

An appeal was lodged. Public interest waxed high. A special Service of Intercession was held in Liverpool Cathedral that God might guide the Court of Criminal Appeal to a right decision.

And then—the unbelievable happened! For the first time in the entire history of British Law the court allowed a murder appeal on the grounds that the verdict had been against the weight of the evidence, and Wallace walked out of the Old Bailey into that freedom which he must have almost ceased to believe possible for him.

But the dark forces which had gathered, like so many low, menacing storm-clouds, about Wallace's life were not so easily dispelled. Legally free, he found himself lonely and outcast as any convicted prisoner. Backs were turned upon him, smiles froze and eyes glazed where only amiable acquaintanceship had been before. He left Anfield and retired to a small cottage in Cheshire, and, just two years later, he died in Clatterbridge Hospital of renal cancer at the age of fifty-four. He protested his innocence to the last and it is difficult for us to reach any satisfactory conclusion, for the most extra-ordinary thing about the Wallace case is that every piece of evidence is capable of bearing two diametrically opposed, yet equally convincing, interpretations—the sinister and the innocent.

It was, perhaps, a very significant comment which was made to me by a man who knew Wallace personally, and who was present at the City Café on that fateful January evening in 1931. "The more I study the evidence," he said, "the more I am inclined to think that Wallace *must* have done it; and yet the more I think of Wallace as I knew him, the less likely I think it that he *did* in fact do it."

It seems that whichever way one turns in the maze of intrigue which surrounds the death of Julia Wallace, the mind finds itself perpetually in check and reason struggles incessantly in the throes of a real-life problem that must always end in an irresolvable stalemate.

11. MOTIF IN FLY-PAPERS

When first I beheld it in the fast fading light of a late May evening, Battlecrease House looked very much like any other of the solid, respectable relics of the mid-Victorian period which flaunt their nostalgic opulence in the face of austere modernity. Nothing, save the lingering memories of the rearguard of an almost lost generation, now remains to hint at the one-time mystery which centred upon it. All was silence. The old house seemed to know peace at last. I sat within its grounds upon a quaint garden-seat. The mauve of the lilac, the gold of the laburnum, and the emerald-green lawn set in a border of sapphire-blue flowers, all lent an air of perfect tranquillity to the scene. In a nearby bush an evening bird began to voice a vesperal, sharp and clear above the low-pitched insect chorale, droning, insistent and drowse-compelling.

My thoughts began to wander. The mind, all unconsciously, bridged the gap of time back over the dusty irredeemable years of almost a century.

★　★　★　★

On such a night as this, nearly a hundred years ago, tragedy had come to Battlecrease House. Within its foursquare walls a man lay dying. Voices were hushed, anxious faces watched and waited. Suddenly the weak breathing stopped; a sheet was drawn over pale, collapsed features that twitched no longer. Silent figures, moving on toe-tips, left the bedside. A dry rustle quivered upon tense air as the blind was gently pulled down. The drama of a life had seen its climax and its close. It was as if that drawing down of a blind was the signal for the raising of the curtain upon another drama, the terrible drama of a woman's fight for life, for at that very moment the ugly thought of murder was ousting from the minds of the death-bed vigilants the chastening realisation that Death had passed amongst them.

In the next room a young woman lay prostrate, senseless upon the crumpled cover of her bed. She knew nothing of the passing of her husband and a merciful oblivion yet screened her from the harsh voices that had begun to cry "Murderess" in a unison of hate. This is our first glimpse of the twenty-six-year-old widow of the wealthy, middle-aged Liverpool cotton merchant. A few weeks later she will stand in the dock accused of his murder and the name of Florence Elizabeth Maybrick will be blazoned throughout the length and breadth of England, the echoes of her shame reverberating through the long, misty corridors of futurity.

Her story is simple enough. A young wife and a husband, twenty-four years her senior, who is the slave of drug-borne fantasy. He neglects her;

51

she resents it and, being human, seeks solace and understanding in the arms of another. There is the triangle; there the motive. The husband dies in questionable circumstances: she it was, they say, who brought about his death. Nor was opportunity lacking, for it is by no means unknown for the ministering angel of the sick-room to turn assassin and hide beneath the cloak of tender devotion, the swift-despatching poison-cup. Add to this discovery of her clandestine liaison, and vague suspicion rapidly crystalizes into conviction and the dread verdict is pronounced. What, then, is so unusual about this? Wherefore this nation-wide clamour? It is the old, old story of the delight of the empty-headed vulgar in any revelation of impropriety in high places. The merest crumb of scandal that falls from the regal table affords a veritable feast to the scavengers who thrive upon such carrion. With what interested satisfaction did these despicables learn that the surface calm at Battlecrease House masked but thinly a muddy depth of misery and intrigue. The wealthy, charming, and eminently respectable James Maybrick of the smug suburb of Aigburth stood revealed as a brutal, faithless drug-addict, and his gentle, refined wife as a murderess, and, worse than that, the willing paramour of another man! How delicious a morsel to add to the dainty fare at the tables of the chattering bevies of tea-takers in drawing-rooms where the Maybricks had once been honoured guests.

It was in 1881 that James Maybrick's business had taken him to America, and it was upon a liner in the vast Atlantic waste that he came upon his destiny in the pretty face and petite form of the girl who was to become his wife. What helpless puppets were these two in the hands of the strange fate that brought them together. Born the wide world apart, she among Alabama's waving fields of cotton, and he within the forbidding shadow of Lancashire's dark, satanic mills, it was their pre-ordained lot to shape each act and point each wandering step to this inevitable end. Did they, one wonders, ever for a brief moment read beyond life's meaning the omen of death's advent in each other's eyes? Or did they hold but love and promises of an eternal season of wine and roses? On July 27th, 1881, they were married at St. James's Church, Piccadilly. For a couple of years they lived at Norfolk, Virginia, returning to England in 1884 to take up residence at Battlecrease House, in Aigburth's Riversdale Road. Here they lived, happily enough for a time, in a manner befitting their wealth and station. They moved in the best circles of Liverpool Society, rode, went to the races, dances and soirées. In 1886 a little girl was born (they had had a boy in 1882) and the Maybricks were regarded by all and sundry as an exceptionally happy and well-favoured couple.

But the dark, ragged clouds that precurse the storm were fast gathering upon their horizon. There were many long, lonely nights when the young wife sat alone in the sombre remoteness of her heavily-furnished drawing-room, always listening for the sound of a key in the lock which never came. Gay and vivacious, such solitude weighed sadly upon her spirits.

All her efforts to immerse herself in the diversions of reading and needlework were of no avail and she fell a helpless victim of the toils of *ennui*. It was about this time also that she discovered that the man in whose hands she had placed her life was consistently unfaithful to her, and was, moreover, a drug-addict. Such was the state of affairs when she met young Alfred Brierly.

He was superficially charming, and seemed kind and considerate—the very antithesis of her bucolic husband, who was becoming increasingly unpleasant daily. Fickle flattery did its insidious work, the lonely heart fancied that it had found sympathetic companionship at last, and, for a time, rejoiced. But the way ahead was not the primrose path of joy; for her the road of thorns. Her felicity was short-lived, reaching its pathetically sordid crescendo in a "daring" three-day sojourn with Brierley at an obscure London hotel, whither she escaped in March 1889, on the pretext of paying a dutiful visit to an invalid aunt.

There is no evidence that Maybrick suspected her affair with Brierley, but nevertheless he was the cause of a very unpleasant scene. It came about in this way.

On March 28th, Mrs. Maybrick returned from her illicit interlude, and on the following day accompanied her husband to the Grand National Steeplechase at Aintree. There, they happened to meet Brierley, and Mr. Maybrick appears to have resented the attentions which the latter paid to his wife. A public scene ensued, and upon their return to Battlecrease House, there was a violent altercation, Maybrick so far forgetting himself as to give his wife a black-eye. It seems that he also availed himself of the opportunity to tax her with her extravagance. As a result of this quarrel Mrs. Maybrick expressed her intention of leaving the house that very night, but her husband told her that if she did so he would never again permit her to see her children. She decided, therefore, to take no action until the following day. The next morning, however, she went to see the family physician, Dr. Hopper, to ask his advice concerning the institution of divorce proceedings. He was opposed to the idea of a separation and agreed to see Maybrick and talk the position over with him. The good doctor's intervention brought about a reconciliation, for James Maybrick undertook to discharge his wife's liabilities to the tune of £1,200, while she for her part, stated that was prepared to forgive and forget. But there can be little doubt that from this day forward James Maybrick's death-warrant was sealed.

On April 13th, Maybrick departed for London. The purpose of his visit was twofold. He wished to see his brother Michael Maybrick (better known to posterity as Stephen Adams, composer of many popular songs) regarding Mrs. Maybrick's financial redemption, and he also wished to consult his brother's physician, Dr. Fuller, concerning the state of his health. It may be mentioned at this point that James Maybrick was pronouncedly hypochondriacal. He was constantly experiencing the most distressing aches and pains which he tended to interpret in even more distressing terms of disease. His pet phobia was creeping paralysis, and a certain numbness in his head and extremities, which he frequently experienced, unfailingly produced the firm conviction that the paralysis had got him at last! He was an inveterate patent-medicine swallower, always prepared to advise or be advised on the latest nostrums. Dr. Fuller was unable to discover any symptoms of serious organic disorder, attributed Maybrick's discomfort to dyspepsia, and prescribed accordingly. He returned to Liverpool on April 22nd, much relieved mentally.

It was on either the 23rd or 24th of April that Florence Maybrick went to the shop of Mr. T. S. Wokes, the local chemist, and bought a dozen fly-papers for sixpence. This purchase was made quite openly and after making some commonplace remark concerning the troublesomeness of flies in her kitchen, she requested Wokes to send his boy with them to Battlecrease House. These fly-papers were never used for the purpose for which they were supposedly intended. Indeed, we have the evidence of the servants that there were at that particular time no noticeable numbers of flies present in the kitchen. On or about April 24th, two of the servants observed in Mrs. Maybrick's room a basin which was covered with a towel. Curiosity overcoming them, they removed this towel and found beneath it another smaller basin, also covered by a towel, which proved to contain some fly-papers soaking in a quantity of water. This fact becomes very significant when we learn that each of these fly-papers contains somewhat over two grains of arsenic, which can be extracted quite easily by the simple expedient of soaking them, and that two grains constitutes a fatal dose of that substance. A day or two later, Mr. Maybrick is coming downstairs; a horrible faintness overcomes him; he reels, his head begins to swim, and he feels that dreaded numbness in his legs again. He grits his teeth and sets off for his office. Somehow or other he gets through that morning, and by lunch-time he is feeling so much better that he decides to attend the Wirral races. In view of the inclemency of the weather this was rather rash, and when he arrived home that evening he was wet through. Nevertheless, he insisted on keeping a dinner engagement with some friends. The dinner was not a success as he felt poorly. He was home before 9 o'clock and went to bed. As he was no better in the morning,

Dr. Humphreys was summoned and he advised the discontinuance of some medicine which Maybrick was taking and which contained strychnine. The next day Mrs. Maybrick made another of those curious purchases of fly-papers for non-existent flies. This time she went to the shop of Mr. Christopher Hanson in the neighbouring district of Cressington. Here she bought a bottle of cosmetic lotion and a further two dozen arsenic-impregnated fly-papers.

Mr. Maybrick is now on the mend and by the evening of April 30th, is so far recovered that his wife is able to attend a private Domino ball at Wavertree with her brother-in-law, Edwin Maybrick. This ball is an important event in the history of the case, for it was claimed by Mrs. Maybrick to supply the motive for her bizarre shopping. She said that from her earliest childhood she had suffered from a most unfortunate periodic irritation of the skin of her face which she believed to be due to some gastric disorder. When she was at school in Germany, a friend had given her the receipt for a face-lotion which would swiftly remove many of the little blemishes which were so ruinous to her complexion. One of the ingredients in this lotion was arsenic, but her school-friend had told her that the very small quaintity required could be extracted quite easily from soaked fly-papers. At the time of the Wavertree Domino ball, her face was in a state of uncomfortable irritation, and it was in order to prepare the balming lotion that she had procured the fly-papers.

By Mayday, James Maybrick was sufficiently recovered to return to his work, but as he still felt rather too weak to wander round cafés he took with him for his lunch some Barry's "Revalenta Arabica," a farinaceous food for invalids, which the cook had prepared for him in a jug given to her by Mrs. Maybrick. This made him sick and he ascribed his indisposition to the cook having put some inferior sherry in the mixture. Traces of arsenic were subsequently found in that jug. The next day he again lunched on the "Revalenta" and was again violently sick. By the evening of May 3rd, he was in great pain and Dr. Humphreys was summoned once more. During the next three or four days, Maybrick's condition was very unsettled. At first it seemed as though he was going to recover, but by the 7th he was so much worse that Mrs. Maybrick called in Dr. Carter for a second opinion. She also telegraphed for a nurse. It was on that afternoon that the children's nurse, Alice Yapp, saw her mistress apparently pouring medicine from one bottle to another. This struck her as being very peculiar and she began to regard Mrs. Maybrick with something akin to suspicion. The next day she had a hunt around and found a packet which was labelled "Arsenic" in Mrs. Maybrick's trunk. Its presence in that house is one of those mysteries which was never solved. Yapp communicated the discovery to a Mrs. Briggs, an old friend of James Maybrick, who was not slow to apprise his brother Edwin of the fact that in her opinion all was not well at Battlecrease House. Thus were the seeds of suspicion sown and they were speeded in their germination by a letter which Mrs. Maybrick gave to Yapp to post on the afternoon of May 8th. This letter was addressed to "A. Brierley, Esq." The nursemaid opened it and found that it contained the ominous words— "He is sick unto death." In view of the fact that the doctors were not unduly perturbed by the patient's condition at this time, it was surely a rather curious statement. The letter was handed to Edwin Maybrick and from that time onwards Mrs. Maybrick was not permitted to attend her husband.

It was on the evening of May 11th that James Maybrick died. His relatives had all been summoned that morning. The doctors abandoned hope, yet he lingered on throughout that May day, and it was not until 8-30 p.m. that he breathed his last. Mrs. Maybrick had fainted before the end came and remained unconscious for many hours. The corpse had scarce grown cold before a search was made for further arsenic. Arsenic there was, and in abundance. They found traces in Mrs. Maybrick's clothes, amongst the dead man's effects, and in medicines, where, according to the prescriptions, no arsenic should have been. On May 14th, Mrs. Maybrick was arrested. Until then she had been too ill to be charged. She was taken first to the little old-fashioned police-station which still stands in Lark Lane, and thence to Walton Gaol to await her trial, which opened on July 31st, 1889, at St. George's Hall, Liverpool. The trial lasted for seven days. Sir Charles Russell, Q.C., was briefed for the defence.

The evidence of the servants and the chemists told strongly against Florence Maybrick, as did that of her brother-in-law Michael Maybrick. She herself gave evidence from the dock and explained about the face-lotion, swearing that it was for this purpose that she had endeavoured to extract the arsenic from the fly-papers. A number of witnesses testified as to the drug-swallowing propensities of the deceased and stated that no one could be reasonably surprised at anything which was found in his stomach, one witness referring to it as a "druggist's waste-pipe." The medical men disagreed too. The Home Office expert, Dr. Stevenson, said that there was no doubt that Maybrick had died of arsenical poisoning, whilst another eminent toxicologist was equally emphatic that arsenic had nothing to do with his death. In view of all this conflicting testimony it seems extraordinary that the jury should have brought in a verdict of guilty, but it was undoubtedly the judge's summing-up which turned them against the prisoner. Before sentence was passed upon her, Mrs. Maybrick in a tensely dramatic moment cried out, "I was guilty of intimacy with Mr. Brierley, but I am not guilty of this crime." The judge donned the black cap, and the dread words of the death sentence echoed through the strained silence of the court. Then Florence Elizabeth Maybrick was led away to Walton Gaol to await the execution of that sentence upon her. Up to the time of the passing of sentence, public opinion had been very much against Mrs. Maybrick, but no sooner had pronouncement been made, than it veered in her favour in the most astounding way. The judge was jeered and cat-called as he left St. George's Hall, newspapers throughout the country condemned the conduct of the trial, protest meetings were held and petitions for a reprieve poured in to the Home Secretary. As a result of this nation-wide clamour she was reprieved from the gallows which she herself had heard being erected at Walton. Her sentence was commuted to one of life imprisonment, and she spent fifteen years in Aylesbury and Woking prisons. On her release in 1904, she went to America and produced a book entitled *My Fifteen Lost Years*—surely the only book of its kind ever written. On the 24th October, 1941, Mrs. Maybrick died, aged 80 years, at South Kent, Connecticut, but not before she had revisited Liverpool and seen the Grand National in 1927. Now, the last of the actors in that memorable Victorian tragedy is dead, but there will be no hurried forgetting of her name. She rests, we hope, in peace, and has taken her secret with her. There will be no rest for us who remain, for the problem of whether she was a woman who did wrong, or a woman wronged, lingers still to tantalize the minds of those who find an interest in such mysteries.

★　　★　　★　　★

Gradually my mind came back to the present. I began to feel a wind that blew a little chill. Evening had slipped into the cloak of night as surely and silently as the heat and haze of high noon fade into the mellow glow of late afternoon. Nightfall, and I was alone in this isolated place, the domain of ghosts, and yet I felt no fear, only peace. Gone was the babble of curious tongues; gone the jostling throng of morbid sightseers. Before me stretched the long gravel drive down which the body of James Maybrick was carried in the great hearse, with its waving black ostrich-plumes, on that final journey to the last abode of crumbling mortality at Anfield. All this had happened so long ago that the veneer of horror seemed to have been worn off by the restless hand of time. The wind rustling the leaves of a copper-beech murmured secrets that no man can know. A few wisps of fog from the nearby river swirled among the trees and made ghost-like wraiths upon the yellowing facade of Battlecrease House. Somewhere in the distance a dog barked, a fog-horn moaned the pleading of a ship's soul. I drew my coat closer about me and stepped forth into the darkness leaving the old house to the vague entities that seem still to cling to its brooding walls on such a night.

12.   HOW DEATH CAME TO FLORENCE MAYBRICK

On August 7th, 1889, a woman stood in the dock of the Crown Court at St. George's Hall and heard the dread sentence of the law passed upon her.

The woman's name was Florence Elizabeth Maybrick and she had been accused of the murder of her husband at their home in Aigburth. Her story has been told and retold many times, but over the years it has gathered about itself that aura of fascination which frequently attaches to things which belong to the past. Moreover, it bears a burden of nostalgia which in these hectic days recalls pleasurably a leisured age of crinolines and carriages when Aigburth was virtually a country village which the brick tentacles of Liverpool had yet to engulf.

Was Mrs. Maybrick guilty? That was the question which, ninety-six years ago, divided all England. A jury decided that she was, but the great British public felt that there was some doubt in the matter. Petitions, signed by thousands of people, began to flood into the Home Office. Largely as a result of this agitation, the Home Secretary was persuaded to re-examine the evidence, and, on August 22nd, 1889, he commuted her sentence to one of penal servitude for life.

As prisoner P29, the unfortunate Mrs. Maybrick served fifteen years in Woking and Aylesbury prisons. Her term of imprisonment, with full remission for good conduct, was due to finish on July 25th, 1904. In the January of that year she was released on the condition that she spent the next six months in a convent at Truro. At the end of those six months she left England and joined her mother, the Baroness von Roques, at Rouen. Three weeks later she travelled to Belgium and embarked from Antwerp on the steamship *Vaderland* for America. On August 23rd, 1904, just twenty-three years after she had set forth on that fatal voyage in the course of which she had met James Maybrick, she sailed into New York harbour. The girl from Mobile, Alabama, was home.

In the December of 1904, Mrs. Maybrick published in America a book—*My Fifteen Lost Years*. Today a collector's piece, it is surely the only book of its kind ever written. For a while after her return to the States, she tried to lecture, chiefly about conditions in English prisons. But it did not go down too well. A new world had grown up during the long years that she had spent in prison; a world that was not specially interested in the misfortunes of Florence Maybrick. Eventually, tiring of publicity, she settled down in Florida. Sometime later she moved to Highland Park, Illinois, and then . . . she just disappeared.

Now, as a result of certain information which chance has put into my hands, I am able to tell the full story of how, more than half a century after she was condemned to die, death came to Florence Maybrick.

The year is 1923. The scene shifts to a tiny, three-room shack in the woodlands of the Berkshire Foothills, between the villages of Gaylordsville and South Kent, Connecticut. A stranger has just moved into this little rural community. A small, thin, bent woman with a face as wrinkled as a walnut, she calls herself Mrs. Florence Chandler. Shortly after her arrival, a neighbour, Mrs. Austin of Gaylordsville, does her several kindnesses. Mrs. Chandler is grateful and makes her a present of a dress. One day Mrs. Austin is shaking that dress and from the shoulder-padding there drops a cleaner's card. Upon it are written the tell-tale words "Mrs. Florence Maybrick, Highland Park, Ill." The secret is out. But, for once, that luck which seems so rarely to have favoured Mrs. Maybrick, is attending her. Mrs. Austin tells her sister of her discovery and together they consult a local woman probation officer. There is a family council, just the three ladies and the husbands of the two sisters. Gallantly they resolve to forego the temptation to release upon the church-socials and the staid bridge-parties the juciest morsel of gossip of a lifetime.

So it was that five charitable people made a vow of silence and Mrs. Maybrick was permitted to spend the last twenty years of her life unrecognised and unpersecuted.

As the years slipped by, the shy, scurrying little old lady became a well-known character of the local scene. They nicknamed her "Lady Florence." She spent most of her time on the campus of the South Kent School, a quaint figure in her one, indestructible, brown straw-hat, a gunny sack slung over her meagre shoulder. Into this sack were stuffed newspapers—old copies of the *New York Times* and an occasional *Bridgeport Sunday Post*—which, salvaged from academic dustbins, made up her only reading. The sack also contained little titbits for cats, for Mrs. Chandler had developed an immence passion for those creatures and her days were mainly devoted to looking after their welfare. Indeed, she was known to successive generations of South Kent boys as "The Cat Woman."

From time to time there were rumours, rumours of the sort that always circulate about lonely old ladies who live secluded lives, that she had been left a vast fortune. Perhaps she did receive some small legacy, for in 1927 she was able to revisit Liverpool and attend the Grand National. It seems fairly certain, however, that towards the end she was very poor having nothing but an old-age pension. With advancing age she became rather eccentric. No one was ever allowed to enter her shack which was always in a state of dirt and disarray. And all through the night she kept burning a single, twinkling light. It was as if she feared ghosts which the darkness might raise from out the grave of a past which she wished

13. THE ARCHER-SHEE CASE

One small boy against the British Empire.

That was the Archer-Shee case.

It was one autumn morning in the year 1908 that a slender envelope plopped through the letter-box of the home of Mr. Martin Archer-Shee, a Liverpool bank-manager, and utterly shattered that gentleman's matutinal composure.

The message which it contained was brief and to the point. It came from the commandant of the Royal Naval College at Osborne where his 13-year-old son, George, had, a few months before, been accepted as a cadet. The Lords Commissioners of the Admiralty deeply regretted that George Archer-Shee would have to be dismissed.

The circumstances which compelled the authorities to this unhappy decision centred upon the theft of a five-shilling postal order from the locker of one of the other young cadets. Having digested the contents of this bombshell, Archer-Shee the elder, hardly waiting to digest his breakfast, departed posthaste for the Isle of Wight and confronted his son.

"Did you do this thing?"

With tears in his eyes, George vehemently denied that he did. His father believed him. The commandant and My Lords Commissioners were challenged by the affronted father.

They gave no direct replies to the anxious parent's continually reiterated enquiries but remained obstinately immovable in their decision that the boy must be withdrawn from the College. Martin Archer-Shee squared his jaw and determined to make a fight of it. George, meanwhile, was returned to his old school, Stonyhurst, and a family council of war was held, with Mr. Archer-Shee's eldest son, who happened to be an M.P, a Major and a holder of the D.S.O., promising his fullest support.

The campaign was opened with a flourish by the retaining of that justiciary giant, Sir Edward Carson. Before agreeing to act in the case at all, Carson had a personal interview with young Archer-Shee. He heard the full story from the boy's own lips and subjected him to a fierce cross-examination of that same deadly ilk which had, thirteen years before, reduced even the lance-witted Oscar Wilde to bewildered collapse. Young Archer-Shee apparently came out well in this unnerving ordeal, and from that point onwards Sir Edward devoted all of his very considerable forensic skill to the service of what he passionately believed to be a sadly-wronged boy.

The first thing to be done, said Carson, was to get the case into court. Ordinarily, there would have been no difficulty about that, but when he became a naval cadet George Archer-Shee had forfeited the rights of normal citizenship without receiving in their place the status which entitled him to demand a court-martial.

Sir Edward locked himself up in his chambers and thumbed his way through a mountain of legal literature. When at length he emerged, he had discovered a solution to the problem. The only chance lay in taking advantage of the rusty legal mechanism known as the Petition of Right. In order to do this, he had first to establish the idea that there had been a violation of contract. Briefly, this involved the allegation of failure on the part of the Crown to keep the bargain implicit in the binding agreement between, on the one hand, the boy, who had undertaken to serve as an officer in the Navy once he had completed the necessary training, and, on the other hand, the Crown, which had, in respect of a substantial payment on the boy's behalf, undertaken to provide the aforesaid training. Irrespective, however, of the existence or non-existence of a contract, a subject is only permitted to sue the King under certain conditions, chief amongst which is the provision that His Majesty must consent to write across the Petition of Right "Let right be done." Whether or not, in the case of the Archer-Shee Petition, Edward VII, always a great sportsman, did actually write those vital words in his sprawling hand right across the document is a moot point, but in any event he gave his assent. Naturally, this rather forced the Admiralty's hand and the Justices to whom a demurrer was carried on appeal requested that they be put in possession of the facts. That, of course, was precisely what Sir Edward Carson wanted to do, and when, in July 1910, nearly two years after the stealing of the postal order, the trial took place, Carson had won the first round in his battle to "Let right be done."

At this stage, moreover, the case had moved out of the category of a personal shindy between an irate father and an obdurate Admiralty, to become an issue of national interest and import. On that hot July morning when Sir Edward Carson rose to his feet to address the court in behalf of the Suppliant, not only a crowded public-gallery but, in column after closely-printed column of newspaper reports, a whole Empire was following the progress of the case.

"A boy thirteen years old," said Sir Edward, "was labelled and ticketed, and has been since labelled and ticketed for all his future life, as a thief and a forger, and in such investigation as led to that disastrous result, neither his father nor any friend was ever there to hear what was said against a boy of thirteen, who by that one letter, and by that one determination was absolutely deprived of the possibility of any future career either in His Majesty's Service, or indeed in any other Service. Gentlemen, I protest against the injustice to a little boy, a child of thirteen years of age, without communication with his parents, without his case ever being put, or an opportunity of its ever being put forward by those on his behalf—I protest against that boy at that early stage, a boy of that character, being branded for the rest of his life by that one act, an irretrievable act that I venture to think could never be got over. That little boy from that day, and from the day that he was first charged, up to this moment, whether it was in the ordeal of being called in before his commander and his captain, or whether it was under the softer influences of the persuasion of his own loving parents, has never faltered in the statement that he is an innocent boy."

Bit by bit, the whole sorry story came out, and in the light of probing justice it stood revealed as something more than one person's fight to re-establish his good name. In a sense, the small boy in the witness-box ceased to matter. Wider issues were at stake: it was a test-case of that sanctity of the individual which is the basis of all the proud boasts of British liberty.

Witnesses told how Cadet Terence Back discovered the loss of his precious postal order, and duly reported it to the Cadet Gunner who, in turn, reported it to the Chief Petty Officer. The post-office was telephoned and the postmistress, Miss Anna Clara Tucker, volunteered that the order had already been cashed. There had, she remembered, been two of the cadets in her post-office that morning. One bought two postal orders totalling 14/9d., the other bought a postal order for 15/6d. She could not recall either of their faces—the cadets all looked alike to her in their uniforms—but she thought that the one who purchased the 15/6d. order also cashed the order for five shillings. Her records showed that the boy who bought the 15/6d. order was Cadet Archer-Shee. As a matter of fact, Archer-Shee admitted buying the 15/6d. postal order. He had that very morning drawn sixteen shillings from some money which he had on deposit with the Chief Petty Officer, in order to send off for a model engine after which he had been hankering for some time.

It was upon the evidence of the postmistress that the authorities condemned young Archer-Shee, and this despite her inability to pick him out at an identity parade to which she was afterwards invited at the College. The testimony of a so-called handwriting expert was scarcely more convincing, and there was no escaping the fact that Archer-Shee had no *need* to steal five shillings. He was amply provided with funds and had only to write a chit in order to secure any sum within reason. Moreover, on the morning in question he had openly requested permission to go out to the post-office and had hung about for some time in the hope of persuading a fellow-cadet to go there with him for company. Were either of these actions compatible with the notion of a cunning young thief tiptoeing furtively off to collect his plunder?

Under the artfully gentle persuasion of Sir Edward Carson, the flustered postmistress now admitted that she had never said that it *was* Cadet Archer-Shee who had cashed the stolen postal order. Nor could she even be sure, now that she came to consider it, that the five-shilling postal order had been cashed by the same cadet who bought the 15/6d. order. That was it. Sir Edward Carson had won. And when on the morning of the fourth day of the trial the court assembled, Sir Rufus Isaacs, the Solicitor-General, jumped to his feet and announced:

"As a result of the evidence that has been given during the trial that has been going on now for some days, and the investigation that has taken place, I say now, on behalf of the Admiralty, that I accept the statement of George Archer-Shee that he did not write the name on the postal order, and did not cash it, and consequently that he is innocent of the charge."

Hearing this, Sir Edward turned round to congratulate the boy himself ... he was nowhere to be seen. George Archer-Shee had overslept and was not in court at the moment of his triumphant vindication!

"Were you not worried?" asked Sir Edward, who himself had lost a good deal of sleep over the possible outcome of the case, when, later, young Archer-Shee went to thank the great advocate in his chambers.

"Oh, no, sir. I knew all along that once the case got into court the truth would come out."

There was the raw material of great drama in the Archer-Shee case, a fact fully appreciated by Terence Rattigan, who was subsequently to use it as the basis of his inspiring play "The Winslow Boy."

As for the *dramatis personæ* of its real-life model, the father lived— but only by a few months—to enjoy the defeat of the bureaucracy and receive a payment of £7,120. And the boy himself? Well, he abandoned all ambitions towards a naval career. In 1914 he was working for a Wall Street firm in America. When the Great War broke out he returned to England and died at Ypres during the first October of hostilities—as a soldier! And there, in the mud of Flanders, ended, at the age of nineteen, the career of Second-Lieutenant George Archer-Shee of the South Staffordshire Regiment.

One small boy against the British Empire. And the small boy won.